MIDDLE EASTERN SKETCHES

Mark N. Katz

University Press of America, Inc.
Lanham • New York • Oxford

Copyright © 1997 by
University Press of America,® Inc.
4720 Boston Way
Lanham, Maryland 20706

12 Hid's Copse Rd.
Cummor Hill, Oxford OX2 9JJ

All rights reserved
Printed in the United States of America
British Library Cataloguing in Publication Information Available

Library of Congress Cataloging-in-Publication Data

Katz, Mark N.
Middle East sketches / Mark N. Katz.
p. cm.
1. Middle East--Description and travel. 2. Katz, Mark N.--Journeys--
Middle East. I. Title.
DS49.7.K38   1997   915.604'52--dc21   97-14071 CIP

ISBN 0-7618-0776-4 (pbk: alk. ppr.)

♾™ The paper used in this publication meets the minimum
requirements of American National Standard for information
Sciences—Permanence of Paper for Printed Library Materials,
ANSI Z39.48—1984

To Toudh

Contents

Preface	vii
In Search of Oman	1
Egyptian Interlude	17
Yemen on My Mind	35
Saudi Sojourn	49
Kuwaiti and Non-Kuwaiti	73
In the Land of Saddam	83
In a Tehran Taxi	101
Moroccan Dialogue	129
A Dip in the Gulf	139
Hopes and Fears	149

Preface

Before visiting there for the first time in 1982, I never expected to become particularly interested in the Middle East. Nor did I did think back then that I would ever make more than one trip to the region.

I was a specialist on the Soviet Union, after all, not the Middle East. I say "I was" a Soviet specialist because it no longer makes much sense to say I am one, there being no Soviet Union left to specialize on. Those of us who were specialists on it are still not certain what we should call ourselves.

But this is getting off the subject. What got me on the subject of the Middle East back in 1982 was a grant from the Rockefeller Foundation to write a book on Soviet foreign policy toward the Arabian Peninsula. This is a topic that has absolutely no importance now, but back then it seemed vital to understand with the Cold War at its height. Curiously enough, while there had been an extraordinary number of books written about Moscow and the seemingly unending Arab-Israeli conflict, there had been precious little written about Soviet foreign policy toward the oil rich Arabian Peninsula countries which the West was so heavily dependant on. Enter me, then, with my proposal for a book on the subject which the Rockefeller Foundation was kind enough to support.

The grant was for twenty-seven months and included some money for travel. I spent more time during the initial three months of the grant organizing my first trip to the Middle East than actually doing research. And it was hard work. Just the logistics of airline and hotel reservations were difficult to arrange. Obtaining visas was also a real challenge.

Even after getting into these countries, making appointments to see people turned out to be a slow, tedious business. And when I did succeed in meeting with them, many Arabs were reluctant back then to say anything about the Soviet Union. I realized during that first trip that just sitting down and reading through the U.S. government's daily translations of the Middle Eastern press at a library in Washington would provide much more useful information for my research project than would the typically uninformative interviews--when I could get them--while in the region. And so I spent virtually all day every day in libraries for almost a year after I got back from this first trip to make up for lost time.

On subsequent trips, I did manage to have frank discussions about the Soviet Union with high level officials--often the only people willing to talk about this subject. I discovered that, whatever their country's rhetoric about the USSR might be, these officials did not seem to consider the Soviet Union very important. Much to my surprise, I found that they would ask me about the details of Soviet statements concerning their country or the region as a whole, often admitting that their foreign ministries really didn't follow the Soviets very closely.

I came to realize, though, that while Arab states might not maintain the elaborate governmental and academic capacity for analyzing Soviet foreign and military policy that existed in America, the Arabs as a whole had a profoundly greater understanding of the USSR than Americans did. For during the Cold War, literally hundreds of thousands of Arabs went to the USSR and Eastern Europe for educational and training programs. Especially after the dramatic oil price rise of 1973 when the Arab world became more and more prosperous, the Arabs who went there saw that the Soviet Union was a very poor country--their own countries were significantly richer in many cases. The USSR just did not have the quality and variety of consumer goods which became increasingly available to people in the oil rich states or even in poorer Arab countries.

Further, despite Soviet rhetoric about how Moscow stood firmly with "the Arab states confronting Israel" (a phrase which Soviet propagandists employed frequently), there was no love lost between Arabs and Russians. The Russians, they quickly discovered, were notoriously prejudiced against Muslims. They learned this both from their own personal experience in the USSR as well as from Soviet Muslims they encountered.

While Americans saw the Soviet Union as a mighty superpower, Arabs understood that it had little to offer them except weapons--and even these, they often complained, were inferior to Western ones. Further, while the Arabs found the West to be both attractive and repellant simultaneously, most found the USSR to be nothing but repellant. In addition to Muslim religious objections against Soviet atheism, the Arab world's intimate familiarity with the many failings of the USSR was an important factor in preventing Marxism-Leninism from becoming a powerful movement in the

Arab world.

But while attempting to understand how Arabs viewed the Soviet Union had brought me to the Middle East in the first place, it was not what kept me coming back. Far more than how they fit into the Cold War struggle between Moscow and Washington, I found the Muslim nations of the Middle East to be fascinating in their own right. And for me, much of the fascination stemmed from the fact that these nations are not easy to understand.

The chapters in this book are what I think of as "sketches" drawn from my travels to various countries of the Muslim Middle East. In them, I seek to convey a variety of impressions: the difficulty for a Westerner to penetrate these societies; the range of thoughts I heard Arabs and Iranians express about a variety of issues including politics, religion, international affairs, and relations between men and women; how these societies appear to others who live and work in them such as diplomats and businessmen; and what life is like in these countries generally.

* * *

I am very grateful for the advice and encouragement I have received for this project from Adeed Dawisha of George Mason University; Charles Dunbar of the Cleveland Council on World Affairs; Dale Eickelman of Dartmouth College; Alexandra Hippisley, Lisa Michael, and Ban Saraf--three of my former students; and most of all, Nancy Yinger--my wife.

This book was made possible through the support from many institutions which enabled me to travel to the Middle East: the Emirates Center for Strategic Studies and Research (Abu Dhabi); the Ford Foundation (Cairo); the Institute for Political and International Studies (Tehran); the International Republican Institute; the Iraqi, Kuwaiti, Omani and Saudi Ministries of Information; the Qatari Ministry of Foreign Affairs; and the Rockefeller Foundation.

Absolutely none of these organizations knew that I was writing this book or that they were supporting it. Until relatively recently, neither did I.

In Search of Oman

Oman is not a country that most Westerners know much about. In fact, Arabs from other countries don't know much about it either. But it was reading about Oman that first got me interested in the Middle East.

It was not Oman's being a Middle Eastern country that interested me then. Instead, it was Oman's role in the Soviet-American competition in the Third World that grabbed my attention.

Like so many young Americans in the late 1970s and early 1980s, I fervently hoped that the U.S. would avoid involvement in "another Vietnam." Having studied the USSR and other communist countries, however, I had no illusions about how benevolent Marxist rule would be once Soviet-backed revolutionaries came to power. We had made a major effort to halt the spread of Marxism in Vietnam, and we had failed. And where we made no effort to halt it afterward, Marxist regimes also came to power in a host of Third World countries during the 1970s. Was there nothing we could do to stop this phenomenon?

Oman seemed to provide an answer. For this was a country which had faced a Marxist insurgency from 1965 to 1975. A Marxist regime had come to power in neighboring South Yemen in 1967 which gave sanctuary to the Omani revolutionaries. Through South Yemen, the Omani Marxists were able to obtain military support from the Soviet Union, China, and other communist countries. And Oman had a curmudgeonly ruler who refused to allow his subjects to become educated for fear that they would make demands which he did not care to grant. Nor would he spend any of the country's growing oil wealth to lift his people out of their grinding poverty.

This appeared to be a situation that was ripe for revolution. By 1970, the insurgency had spread from Oman's southernmost province--Dhofar--into northern Oman. It seemed only a matter of time before the People's

Democratic Republic of Oman came into existence.

But something happened which thwarted this dream. In mid-1970, the old sultan was overthrown by his son, Qabus, with the help of the British (Oman had been a British quasi-protectorate since the nineteenth century). The young Sultan Qabus lifted all the petty restrictions maintained by his father and immediately began an ambitious economic development program. He also offered an amnesty to the Marxist rebels. Not only did many of them lay down their arms, but later took them up again to fight on behalf of the sultan against their former comrades. With the help of a relatively small number of British officers as well as troops sent over by the shah of Iran, the sultan's forces completely crushed the insurgency and drove those who did not surrender back over the border into South Yemen.

From reading Soviet accounts about the war in Oman, it was evident that Moscow was surprised by what had happened. From 1969 when articles first began appearing in the Soviet press about Oman until well into 1975, Soviet commentators confidently predicted the downfall of the sultan and the spread of Marxist revolution from Oman to the rest of the oil rich countries on the Arabian Peninsula. When the guerrillas were finally defeated by the end of 1975, the Soviets expressed real shock and outrage: this was just not supposed to happen, according to them.

Clearly, there were some valuable lessons to be derived from the Omani experience. If the U.S could learn from whatever the sultan had done in Oman, we might be able to prevent Marxist revolution from succeeding elsewhere in the Third World. And so I submitted a proposal to the Rockefeller Foundation for a book on Soviet policy toward Oman. The foundation wisely suggested that I broaden the focus of my study to the Arabian Peninsula as a whole. I agreed, and was awarded a twenty-seven month fellowship to undertake the project. But it was Oman that interested me most.

* * *

I embarked on the fellowship in September 1982. I rapidly discovered that there wasn't much information available on Oman, or any of the Arabian Peninsula countries for that matter. So among the first tasks I set for myself was to arrange a five week trip to Oman, Egypt, and North Yemen beginning in December (Rockefeller had generously provided money for travel).

I quickly learned that getting a visa for Oman would not be easy. In fact, Omani embassies abroad could not issue visas. Permission to enter the country had to come from Muscat, the capital, from which potential visitors had to obtain an "NOC," or non-objection certificate.

The Rockefeller Foundation had arranged for me to have an office at the Brookings Institution, the well-known "think tank" located on a tree-lined block of Massachusetts Ave--Washington's "embassy row." Someone told me that across the street at the Johns Hopkins University School of Advanced International Studies (SAIS), there were two Omani graduate students who were also diplomats working at the Omani embassy a few blocks away.

I thought if I got to know these two, I could interest them in my project and they might help me get into their country. I met them each separately. Both of them were very polite, but neither seemed in the least interested in my research. In fact, when I began to tell them about it, they each indicated that they had an urgent appointment of some sort.

I was somewhat confused by this. People from other nations I knew were usually very interested when I told them I was doing research on their country--especially if they were diplomats. This Omani reaction seemed quite puzzling to me. Had I said something wrong?

I called up my dissertation adviser at M.I.T., William E. Griffith, whom I knew had visited Oman--as well as almost every other country in the world. When I told him what happened, he advised me not to bother talking with the Omani diplomats. Instead, I should call the Omani Information Ministry's representative at the embassy, who was not himself an Omani, but a Bulgarian emigre.

When I talked to the gentleman in question on the phone, he agreed to see me at his office. When I met him there, I found him to be friendly, knowledgeable about Oman, and interested in my project. I told him that I was interested in Oman as an example of a successful counter-insurgency effort against Marxist revolutionaries. Perhaps there were lessons that America could derive from the Omani experience which could be applied elsewhere.

He reacted reticently to this. "It is very difficult to apply the experience of one country to others," he said. "Circumstances are very different in each one." Still, he said that if I wrote him a letter, he would pass it along to the Information Ministry in Muscat with a favorable recommendation. I did just this, and after a few weeks was notified that I would indeed be permitted to visit Oman, and that my wife would be able to come with me.

Shortly thereafter, I also received an invitation to attend a reception at the Omani embassy in celebration of Oman's National Day on November 18. Upon arriving, my wife and I stood in line with the other guests before going up to shake hands with the Omani ambassador, who was then Sadek

Suleiman. He was dressed in his formal Omani robes and was wearing an enormous *hunjar* (traditional Omani knife) in an expensive looking sheath and belt around his waist.

After eating our share of the enormous feast that the Omanis had set out and talking with various people, my wife and I decided to leave. The ambassador was still standing in the receiving area. Since there was no longer a line of people waiting to shake his hand, I thought I might talk with him a little. I told him how I was looking forward to going to his country in just a couple of weeks and was about to tell him about my project when he interrupted me.

"You're going to Oman?" he asked unsmilingly. "Who arranged that?"

I replied that it had been arranged through the Bulgarian gentleman in his embassy who worked for the Information Ministry. I was about to say more when he turned away and began talking with someone else.

I was surprised that he did not seem to know about my trip. But perhaps his time was occupied with far more important matters than overseeing requests by scholars to visit his country.

* * *

On December 1, my wife and I set out on our voyage. Oman would be the first Middle Eastern country either of us had ever been to. We flew overnight from Washington to London, furiously visited friends during our fourteen hour layover there, and then flew overnight again to Muscat. We arrived, exhausted, at 7:30 a.m. local time on December 3.

Back in 1982, the new modern version of the Seeb airport had not yet been built. The few of us who got off the British Airways flight (which was going on to Singapore and Sydney) made our way into the terminal. The Omani immigration officers sat at two amazingly tall desks. But before handing our passports to one of them, we all trooped over to a little window to collect our NOCs. Fortunately, ours were there. One American in a cowboy hat was not so lucky. His wasn't there. He started shouting at the man inside the window, and then at everyone else in general, but to no avail.

Although the lines for the immigration officers were short, they moved slowly. In our zombie-like state of exhaustion, we decided that we would not be able to stay on our feet if we waited in line, so we sat down until everyone but the cowboy had gone through. There were birds flying around inside the terminal, chirping away. The noise made a cheerful contrast to the shouting cowboy.

Finally, the lines disappeared. We went to one of the desks and handed up our passports and NOCs. Our passports were stamped and handed back to us; the immigration officers kept the NOCs. After claiming our bags and clearing customs, we found a man in the main terminal carrying a sign with my name. It was our driver from the Ministry of Information. He packed us and our baggage into his gray car with the ministry's seal and drove us to our hotel.

Our hotel, the Intercontinental, was right on the coast and had its own beach. From the balcony of our room, we could see the Indian Ocean and several oil tankers lying close in. We didn't gaze at the view for long on that occasion, but instantly set to work catching up on our sleep instead.

* * *

The next morning, a car and driver from the Information Ministry showed up at eleven o'clock, just as the note we had been handed at the airport said would happen. We were taken to the Information Ministry where a young Englishwoman showed us into a waiting room before the "man in charge" who knew our schedule could see us. We were shortly joined by the foreign editor of a Japanese newspaper and a married couple from California who, we would later divine, were researchers who had lost their jobs and were now trying to sell their services as consultants to the Omanis.

Although we were the first to arrive in the waiting room, we were the last to be seen, thus conveying to us early on the degree of importance to which the Information Ministry assigned us. After an hour, we were finally ushered in to see the "man in charge." This was not an Omani, but an Englishman named Anthony Ashworth. He was middle aged, but very fit. When we first entered his office, he looked at us with an intense scowl; I think we were a lot younger than he expected. But he bade us welcome and we soon got down to business.

Appointments had been arranged for me, he said, at the Defense Ministry, the Economic Development Council, and Petroleum Development Oman. Since I seemed to be interested in rebellions, he said that we would be taken on a day-trip to Nizwa in the interior of northern Oman (where a rebellion had occurred in 1957-59) and on a two-night trip to Salalah in Dhofar (site of the 1965-75 Marxist rebellion). Weather permitting, I would be taken for a helicopter ride to observe the Strait of Hormuz (the narrow waterway between Iran and Oman through which tanker traffic between the Persian Gulf and the rest of the world must pass) and another one while I was in Dhofar to inspect the border between Oman and Marxist South Yemen. All of these trips would be provided by the Omani government.

We were struck by Omani generosity in providing all these trips for us. On my second and third visits to Oman, though, I was also offered trips to Nizwa and Salalah. Someone at the American embassy suggested that the Omani Information Ministry provided these trips less out of a spirit of generosity than a desire to get foreign visitors out of the capital where they would be pestering Ashworth for appointments. Unfortunately, the weather was poor on the days my helicopter rides were scheduled. And they were not offered during my subsequent trips; to cut back on expenses, the Omani government later decided to reserve these flights for VIPs.

I thanked Ashworth for the appointments which had been arranged but asked if I might request a couple of others. He did not seem pleased, but I pressed on anyway.

"Can I sit in on a session of the State Consultative Council?" I asked. This was the body which had recently been created by the sultan (whom Ashworth always referred to as "H.M.") to give him advice. It could not legislate, and its deliberations were limited to the discussion of economic development issues, but compared to some of the other Arab Gulf monarchies, this was progress.

"I'm afraid that's out of the question," Ashworth replied. "The council only meets for a few days in the year, and when it does, its sessions are closed."

Just like the Soviet parliament, I wanted to say but did not: I didn't think Ashworth would appreciate the comparison.

"And how about someone at the Foreign Ministry?" I asked.

Ashworth frowned. "That might be difficult."

Although this did not sound encouraging, I was pleased with the program that had been arranged. A car and driver took us back to our hotel.

* * *

Later in the afternoon, Ashworth or someone from his ministry sent a car to take us on a tour of the capital. We drove from Ruwi--the suburb where our hotel was located--through Muttrah and into Muscat proper, then back again. There was construction going on everywhere. What impressed us was that the Omani government apparently insisted that new buildings be designed with Omani aesthetics in mind.

We stopped near the sultan's palace in Muscat. It was a modern structure which was both dignified and unpretentious. There were several lovely old buildings nearby. We drove through the bustling modern commercial district in Muttrah and then to the old Muttrah *soukh*, or market place. There appeared to be an endless number of narrow alleyways lined with small shops. If our driver had not escorted us, we would not have found our way out of this maze easily. But he seemed to be intimately familiar with it. The shops were grouped together by type of product sold. There were goldsmiths, silversmiths, food merchants, sellers of cloth, sellers of small electric appliances, and all kinds of other shops.

It was mainly Omani men in the *soukh,* but there were many Omani women too. They tended to be short. Unlike elsewhere in the Arabian Peninsula, the long gowns they wore were quite colorful--not plain black. Scarves covered their heads, but their faces were generally uncovered. Nor were they shy and retiring; their voices could easily be heard loudly bargaining with the shopkeepers.

* * *

Our Information Ministry driver took us back to our hotel and drove off. At dinner time, my wife and I decided to eat outside the hotel. The food in the hotel restaurant was fine, but it was expensive and we thought we would soon get tired of ordering from the same menu for lunch and dinner every day. Back then, there were only a handful of restaurants outside the hotels (of which there were also only a handful). We decided to go to one we had heard about--an Indian restaurant called the Tandoor.

We got into one of the cabs at the Intercontinental and took off. After awhile, however, it became apparent that our driver did not know where the Tandoor was--foreigners, we surmised (and they were probably the only ones who used cabs here) generally asked to be taken to ministries, other hotels, the airport, and nowhere else.

The driver stopped to ask someone on the sidewalk for directions. The man seemed to recognize the name of the restaurant and was talking rapidly with our driver.

"Can you understand what they're saying?" my wife asked me.

I had only recently begun studying Arabic. "I'm afraid I can't," I replied.

"Well that's funny," she said, "because I can."

My wife had participated in study-abroad programs both in India and Nepal, and spent many years learning Hindi, Marathi, and Nepali--all of which are related to one another.

It turns out that Urdu--a South Asian language related to Hindi and its cognates--is widely spoken in Oman. During its heyday in the first half of the nineteenth century, Oman controlled a far-flung empire that included Zanzibar and part of the East African coast as well as part of the coast of present-day Pakistan. Even after losing most of this empire in the nineteenth century, Oman continued to rule one coastal town in Pakistan, Gwadar, until 1958. It had become common for Omani men to marry Muslim women from South Asia. The children of these marriages often learned their mother's language--Urdu--first. Hence, Urdu is widely spoken in Oman, especially along the coast. This contributed to Oman seeming more like a South Asian country than an Arab one in many ways.

Armed with the directions, our driver took us to the Tandoor. He was both shocked and overjoyed that my wife was able to communicate with him. Word would spread quickly among both the taxi and Information Ministry drivers as well as the hotel doormen about my wife's linguistic skills. Hence, we became very popular with them.

The restaurant was small and unpretentious, but it served excellent food at very low prices. Afterward, we ended up having to wait over an hour in the dark before catching a taxi back to our hotel, but the experience had been worth it.

* * *

The next day, the Information Ministry took us along with the Californian couple to the offices of Petroleum Development Oman. Here again, the individual we spoke to was not an Omani, but an Englishman. After a largely technical discussion about Omani oil production levels, world oil prices, and other such matters, we were taken back to the hotel. Thus ended the Information Ministry's program for the day.

Fortunately, I had a contact at the American embassy whom we had arranged to see. Our Information Ministry driver was kind enough to drop us off there.

The American embassy was then located near the sultan's palace in an old house leased from a wealthy Omani family. It was cramped and filled with all kinds of twists and turns, but was certainly colorful. One side of the house looked out on one of the two towering fortresses which the Portuguese had built in Muscat during their period of empire. Until recently, this fortress had been used as a prison, and the embassy staff could view the prisoners being led in and out.

We were told to be especially careful going up and down the main staircase in the embassy. Its steps had been deliberately built in uneven lengths. In the past, the owners had held people captive on the upper floor. If they tried to escape, the uneven steps would often lead them to trip and fall in their rush to get out, thereby thwarting their flight. Nice people.

At the embassy, we sensed that the British and the Americans viewed each other as rivals for influence here in Oman, and that the British definitely had the upper hand in the competition. This was not simply due to the close relations between Muscat and London, but to the fact that there were something like eleven thousand British advisers here compared to only about one thousand Americans. The British were everywhere--in the ministries, the oil industry, and even the military.

Ashworth of the Information Ministry was regarded as perhaps the most influential of the British advisers. For not only was he an adviser to the minister of information, but to the sultan himself. He had been here for years and years. And he didn't seem to like Americans very much, we were told.

* * *

That night, we decided to make an excursion to another restaurant. We went to the Golden Oryx, a Chinese restaurant. I telephoned the restaurant in advance to get directions for the cab driver. We made it there without getting lost this time.

The food was fine, but I felt sorry for the owners since the place was almost empty. After we had been there awhile, four British couples came in and sat at a table near us. We couldn't help but overhear their conversation. Two of the couples had been here for some time, while the other two had just arrived. It appeared that the men all knew each other at least slightly, but the two new women did not know each other or anyone else in the group.

Listening to them, my wife and I quietly remarked to each other how different American and British social interaction is. The tremendous sensitivity which has grown up among educated Americans about making remarks that could be interpreted as ethnic or racial slights simply does not exist among our British counterparts. Indeed, much of British humor seems to be based on negative stereotypes about others. Nor do the British appear to be in the least ashamed about it. A large part of our neighbors' conversation consisted of the "old hands" describing the depths of Omani ignorance and incompetence.

* * *

The next morning we found ourselves in the Information Ministry waiting room again with the same people as before: the Japanese journalist and the would-be consultants from California. We were seen by Ashworth again in the same order: first the Japanese, then the Californians, then us. We only had to wait about a half an hour this time, but just as we sat down to talk with

Ashworth, he was suddenly called away by the information minister. He'd try to see us tomorrow, he told us.

From there, the five of us went outside and got on board a small bus which took us to Nizwa in the interior. From Muscat, it was a two hour trip there through dry, hilly country. In and around Nizwa, we visited a date processing plant, an archaeological dig of a two thousand year old village, and the Nizwa *soukh*. While the interior was not as prosperous as the capital, the shops were full of goods imported from Japan and the West. Not only were there plenty of cars in the area, but several car dealerships as well.

We also visited two fortresses. One was the great fort of Nizwa. Parts of it, we were told, were over four hundred years old while other parts were over seven hundred. It was ingeniously designed for defensive purposes. To get to the top, an attacker would have to penetrate seven huge sets of doors. Above six of them was a narrow space from which the defenders could rain down spears, arrows, bullets, or anything else unpleasant on the attackers. At the top of the fortress there was a narrow gateway on the floor from which prisoners were dropped down into a dungeon. Although not in use as a prison for many years, there was a horrible stench at the gateway that made me shudder.

The other fortress had been the headquarters of the imam of Oman and was located outside Nizwa on the approach to the *Jabal Akhdar* (Green Mountain). Control over Oman had long been contested by the imam based in the interior and the sultan based on the coast. In the early part of the twentieth century, the imam's forces had gotten the best of the chronic fighting; the sultanate might have disappeared altogether if the British had not acted to preserve it in Muscat. In 1957-59, however, the imamate was destroyed altogether by Sultan Qabus's father with the help of the British.

Unlike the Nizwa fortress, the imam's was in a state of ruin. The local guide explained to us that in the fight against the old sultan, the fortress had been defended by the imam's daughter since her father was up in the hills. Her defense of the fortress was so fierce and effective that the sultan's men could not capture it. The British Royal Air Force had to be called in to bomb the fortress until it surrendered. Someone later suggested that it had been left in a state of ruin as a deterrent to any other potential opponents of the sultan's rule.

* * *

The next morning, the five of us were again taken to the Information Ministry's waiting room. This time, however, my wife and I were seen first.

But we soon discovered that this was not because Ashworth wanted to make up for keeping us waiting so long yesterday morning only to dismiss us after entering his office. Instead, he was angry.

The Omanis understood that America "is the hope of the free world," he told us patronizingly, but "American gaucherie" frequently damaged U.S. interests and made it difficult for others to cooperate with the U.S. He was "particularly annoyed," he told us, by an Associated Press report that had just come out in which a U.S. Defense Department official was quoted stating that Oman had privately agreed to participate in military exercises with the U.S., but did not want this information to be made public as this would embarrass the Omani government. "Such a leak, of course, has embarrassed Oman in exactly the way it wanted to avoid being embarrassed!"

I thought that his message was intended less for us than it was for the U.S. embassy, which he undoubtedly knew we were in contact with from the Information Ministry driver who had taken us there. The message was duly delivered by us to the embassy later that day. "These Brits fail to understand that we don't exercise the kind of control over our press that they do over theirs," was the response.

After Ashworth had gotten this off his chest, he relaxed a bit. We had a long chat about South Yemen, where he had served in the colonial administration until the British pulled out in 1967. Unlike the Americans, he told me, British forces had won every counter-insurgency struggle they had fought against Marxists. There had been only one exception: South Yemen.

He blamed this loss not on how British armed forces in South Yemen had conducted the war, but on the policy of the British Labour party which was elected to office in 1964. The Labour party essentially abandoned the counter-insurgency effort and handed power to the Marxists in 1967. He was especially bitter about this because, unlike the American public which was averse to protracted military interventions in the Third World, the British public was not. It had long become accustomed to it after literally centuries of British involvement in this kind of warfare. There was no great public demand in Britain to withdraw from South Yemen as occurred in American public opinion with regard to Vietnam. The Labour government gave up the effort more as a cost cutting measure than anything else.

Ashworth and many like him who had served in South Yemen later came to Oman determined to prevent what had happened in the former from occurring in the latter--as seemed highly likely in 1970. Reading the British accounts of the counter-insurgency effort in Oman, it truly is amazing that they were able to prevail with so few men over a guerrilla force that was receiving sanctuary and support through neighboring South Yemen and which had overrun over ninety percent of Dhofar province. Compared to the much larger American involvement in Indochina spanning roughly the same time period, the British achievement in Oman appears more remarkable still.

We talked with Ashworth for about an hour about Marxist insurgencies in Oman, South Yemen, and elsewhere as well as the difference in American and British approaches to them. At the end of the conversation, he actually seemed quite friendly. As we left his office, we suddenly realized that we, for once, had kept everyone else who wanted to see him waiting for an hour.

* * *

Later that day, we and the Californians were taken to the Economic Development Council. This time, we actually got to speak to an Omani. There were, however, plenty of foreigners working there, as we observed from the open doors to offices along the corridors we walked through.

The Californians gave their pitch about the valuable services they could provide to the Omanis. Clearly nonplused, the Omani gave us each a set of statistical compendia about Oman.

My wife, who is a demographer, asked what was the population of Oman. He told us quite forthrightly that while the official Omani government figure was 1.5 million, some international agencies said that it was eight hundred thousand. Here in this office, he said, "One million was considered a reasonable figure." But no one knew for sure since there had not yet been a census.

After the meeting was over, we and the Californians speculated on why the Japanese journalist had not come with us. We all suspected that a much more interesting meeting had been arranged for him to which we had not been invited. We learned later that this was exactly what had happened: he had been granted an interview by Yusuf al-Alawi, the minister of state for foreign affairs. Al-Alawi was an interesting figure because he had been one of the Dhofari rebels who accepted the amnesty offer made by Sultan Qabus shortly after the latter came to power.

We were all seething with jealousy. We wondered what the Japanese journalist had that we didn't have--besides several million readers.

* * *

The next morning, December 8, was unusual in two respects. First, we did not pay a visit to the Information Ministry. Second, we did pay a visit to the

Defense Ministry--something I have never managed to do in any other Middle Eastern country.

In addition to the "gang of five" as we called ourselves, there were several other journalists present: two more from Japan, one from Austria, and one--a lady--from Britain.

An officer from each of the three armed services gave a briefing. For the army, it was a British officer. For the navy, it was also a British officer. For the air force, it was an Omani officer. During the question-and-answer period, however, the Omani did not address any questions about the air force; a British officer did that.

The briefing was highly informative not only because of what was said but who said it. In other countries, the armed forces are the symbol of nationalism and patriotism. I couldn't imagine any other country in which foreigners would be allowed to speak on behalf of the armed forces. Surely just for public relations purposes, I thought, the sultan's government should have had only Omanis give briefings. But this, apparently, was not how the Omani government thought, at least back then.

* * *

The next day, December 9, we flew from Muscat to Salalah, capital of Dhofar. Traveling with us from Muscat were two Egyptian journalists. They were quite talkative and kept up a steady stream of jokes. They made a stark contrast with the quiet, serious Omanis we had met with. But since we hadn't met very many Omanis, we had no idea whether these were personality traits common to the nation as a whole or just to those officials assigned to deal with foreigners.

Ashworth's office told us before we left that we had an appointment to see the provincial governor. As soon as we arrived, however, we were told by the Information Ministry contact there that the governor had just flown to Muscat and thus could not see us. We were not surprised.

The four of us were taken to the Salalah Holiday Inn. The hotel was not actually owned by the hotel chain, but by the government instead. This was just as well for the company's shareholders: we were told that the hotel normally had only a five percent occupancy rate.

In the afternoon, a car and driver came to take my wife and I on a tour of the immediate vicinity. Just a few miles inland from the flat coastal plain rose up the mountainous region--the *jabal*--which the Dhofari rebels had once controlled. As we drove along the winding roads into the hill country, we passed several small military encampments. These were called *firqats;*

they were the bases for rebels who had accepted the sultan's amnesty in the 1970s. These former rebels were still responsible for maintaining security in the hills.

"Can I visit some of the *firqats*?" I asked.
"No," was the reply.
"Why not?"
"They are busy."

I did not see even one person on the grounds of any of the camps that we passed by. Perhaps they were all inside doing their paperwork.

Our driver kept up a running commentary about how Dhofar had benefited so much from the rule of Sultan Qabus. None of the Dhofaris had any admiration for Marxist South Yemen, which they knew had only become poorer while Oman had become richer. Clearly, the fact that we were driving around freely in these hills was proof that there was no longer a war going on here.

After awhile, we drove out of the hills and back into Salalah. After a tour of the shopping district, he dropped us back at the hotel.

It seemed strange that evening walking into the hotel dining room, because we knew each and every one of the diners: in addition to the Egyptians, there were the Californians and the British lady journalist (these three had flown down on a later flight). I think the seven of us were the hotel's only guests.

The next day, a different driver picked us up. He didn't know much English, but we managed to communicate a little in my basic Arabic. He took us along the coastal road toward the border to a fishing village. Tens of thousands of sardine-like fish had been set out on racks to dry in the sun. The smell was quite intense, and so we didn't stay for long.

On the way back, we stopped along the road to look at some camels. Our driver went right up and petted them--something we couldn't quite bring ourselves to do. We then went back to Salalah where we bought some frankincense--which is grown in Dhofar. He took us back to the hotel where we had a late lunch. There was no program for the afternoon, so we sat in our room watching a Hindi film on the in-house video. There were endless twists and turns in its fantastic plot.

The next morning, December 11, we and the Californians were taken to the nearby Omani air force base. We received a briefing both from an army and an air force officer. This time, the army officer was an Omani while the air force one was British. The briefing here was a lot less formal than the one in Muscat, and we learned a lot more.

Today also happened to be Oman's Armed Forces Day. On display were various weapons in the arsenals of the Southern Brigade and the air force base. As visiting VIPs, we were given a private tour of the display. I was surprised to see that some of the artillery was Soviet. I asked the officer in charge (an Omani) whether these had been captured from the rebels, or whether Oman had obtained them from Egypt (which had been closely allied with and heavily armed by Moscow, but switched its friendship to Washington in the 1970s). He refused to answer. In addition, he would not let me photograph the artillery pieces.

After a few minutes, the display was opened to the public and we found ourselves engulfed in a sea of enthusiastic boys and young men all wearing the traditional white *dishdash*. This was the liveliest group of Omanis we had seen on our visit.

At the insistence of Mrs. California, we were taken on a surprise visit to a girls' school. The lady principal led us into a grammar school class. An impromptu performance was put on in which the teachers would shout out questions and the class would all answer by rote. I could not follow what they were talking about, but the children all displayed a lot of energy and enthusiasm.

This was the only occasion on which we had any interaction with Omani females. The teachers, however, were from Sudan, Egypt, or other Arab countries. Only one--the youngest--was an Omani.

* * *

Late in the afternoon, several of us flew back to Muscat. The Information Ministry driver who took us back to the Intercontinental seemed overjoyed to see us again. He, my wife, and I compared various words in Urdu, Hindi, Arabic, and English. The British lady journalist who was in the car with us seemed utterly scandalized that we were talking with a "native."

Back at the hotel, the staff also treated us like long lost relatives. The next day, we were taken back to the airport and flew off to Cairo.

While sitting in the Gulf Air jet, I reflected on the questions I had come to Oman with. Were there any lessons that America could learn from the Omani experience in order to successfully defeat Marxist insurgents and maintain peace afterward? Putting the British in charge of the counter-insurgency effort and letting them run things indefinitely afterward seems to have been the solution that the sultan and his government found satisfactory. And although American diplomats might grouse about the British, it was also the solution that the U.S. government found satisfactory too. I couldn't help but wonder, though, whether or for how long the Omani people would find it satisfactory.

Egyptian Interlude

In addition to Oman, I wanted to go to North Yemen on my first trip to the Middle East. But I soon discovered that while the two countries were relatively close to each other, it was very difficult to fly directly between them. There were only a very few flights, and these could not be confirmed in advance. Although relatively far away from both, it was much easier to fly from Oman to Egypt and then from Egypt to North Yemen. And these flights could be confirmed. Since we wanted to visit Egypt anyway, this is what we did.

When we arrived in Cairo, our Egyptian friend Ahmed--whom we had known from Washington--picked my wife and me up at the airport and drove us to the apartment we were staying at in Garden City--one of Cairo's wealthy enclaves. After helping us with our luggage, he said he would come back in the evening and take us to dinner.

Ahmed arrived at the appointed hour, but without his car. It had broken down, so we would have to take a cab out to the Pyramid Road on the outskirts of town where the restaurant he had selected was located. We had no trouble getting a cab out from Garden City. Trying to come back into town after dinner, however, proved to be more difficult.

We waited half an hour before a taxi appeared. We hailed it, but the driver did not want to take us to Garden City. He lived near the Pyramid Road and was about to quit for the day. He didn't want to have to drive all the way into town and back again at this hour. I couldn't blame him after witnessing Cairo's unbelievable traffic jams earlier. But even our Cairene friend seemed to become anxious about finding another cab as the darkness increased and the temperature dropped on that late December evening.

After another twenty minutes, a second cab appeared. We were much relieved when the driver stopped and said he would take us. Since there was already one passenger riding in the front, Ahmed, my wife and I all crammed into the back of the tiny car. I sat directly behind the driver, my wife in the middle, and Ahmed on the right.

Music was blaring from the car's loudspeakers, one of which was directly behind my head. As we drove off, the driver and his companion in the front seat began (or probably resumed) laughing and shouting. "What is that smell?" asked my wife.

"Hashish," said Ahmed. Hearing that word, the passenger in the front seat offered some to us. We all declined. Our sense of good fortune in having found this cab evaporated quickly as our driver weaved at high speed between the lanes of the major road back into town.

Suddenly, a car darted out from a side street on the left and cut right in front of us. Our driver only avoided hitting it by slamming on his brakes, resulting in the three back seat passengers being shoved up against the front seat. Almost instantly, however, we found ourselves being shoved against the back seat as the driver floored the gas pedal.

Our driver and his friend were cursing and swearing as our taxi overtook the offending vehicle on its right side. I thought we were simply going to speed past him when the taxi driver suddenly rammed the other car. The point of collision for us was the left rear door where I was sitting. The driver and his companion roared in triumph as our taxi sped forward.

The other driver, though, was not going to let this be the final word. He now passed us on the right and rammed us in turn. Both cars came to a halt amid squealing brakes. The two drivers immediately leaped out of their cars and advanced toward each other shouting and brandishing their fists. It looked as if a fight was about to break out.

I had not noticed, but Ahmed had gotten out of the car too. I saw him get between the two men, each of whom was much larger than he. He was talking rapidly while the two continued to make hostile gestures toward each other. Suddenly, the two men threw their arms around each other, kissing one another's cheeks repeatedly. A few seconds later, each driver returned to his car and both took off at a slower pace than before. The two drivers smiled and waved at each other repeatedly until the other car turned off the road onto a side street.

I then asked Ahmed why he had gotten out of the car. "If they had started fighting, you could have gotten hurt."

"But I knew they didn't want to fight," he responded. "They only wanted a mediator.

"In fact," he added, "if I had not gotten out of the car to mediate, they would have had to fight even though they didn't want to."

A couple of days later, I was having lunch at Cairo's Tahrir Club with Mohammad Ezzeldin of the Egyptian Foreign Ministry's Diplomatic Institute. I told him about our experience in the cab and what our friend Ahmed had done to defuse the situation.

Mohammad said that Ahmed's actions were typical of diplomacy among the Arab states. If two states got into a dispute, they would denounce each other as Zionist, imperialist agents. A third state would mediate between them. Afterward, the two parties to the dispute would profess to be the best of friends and blame their quarrel on a nefarious plot by the Zionists and imperialists to "divide the Arab nation."

"When Arab states denounce each other it is mainly just posturing," said Mohammad. "Each side says terrible things, but they really do not expect conflict to result, or to be very damaging even if it occurs. What each side expects is that a mediator will come forward and help them resolve the dispute. In fact, they may denounce each other all the more vehemently because they know that a mediator will step in before anything very serious happens."

"But isn't there a sense," I asked, "that this expression of extreme hate and then extreme love appears ridiculous?"

"It is ridiculous," Mohammad agreed, "but the system works. Eventually, disputes between Arab countries usually get resolved, or at least contained."

I said that I didn't think Westerners could behave like that.

"Maybe not," Mohammad commented, "but when America decides it doesn't like a country, its hatred lasts for years and years. For some reason, you can't go from poor relations to good relations very easily. So while we may look ridiculous to you, you look unbending and inflexible to us. Which is better?"

* * *

One reason why I had wanted to visit Egypt was to do some research there on Yemen. Although it is well known that Egypt has fought four wars with Israel (in 1948, 1956, 1967, and 1973), Egypt also fought a less well known war in North Yemen.

The history of this war is bizarre. In September 1962, the Egyptian leader Nasser sent thousands of his soldiers to North Yemen to help a Nasserist "republican" revolution which had overthrown the country's king. Nasser seemed to hope that the ouster of the Yemeni monarchy would quickly be followed by the demise of the Saudis and the other royal families of the Arabian Peninsula. Instead, the overthrown Yemeni king was able to rally many of the tribes to his cause and put the Yemeni republicans and their Egyptian allies on the defensive.

Even with Soviet military assistance, the Egyptians had to fight hard just to keep the major cities in republican hands. Nasser himself grew disillusioned with the adventure, and at one point in the mid-1960s described Yemen as "Egypt's Vietnam."

In the wake of Israel's rapid defeat of Egypt, Jordan, and Syria in June 1967, Nasser decided he could not afford the Yemeni adventure any longer, and so withdrew his troops. The Yemeni republican cause appeared to be doomed. But then an odd thing happened. As soon as their Egyptian protectors left, the Yemeni republicans grew stronger. They beat back several royalist offensives. The royalist coalition fell apart, and in 1970 the war came to an end. Apparently, a lot of the tribes supporting the royalist cause didn't so much object to the new Yemeni republican government but to the large Egyptian military presence which had come with it.

There is more open discussion of foreign policy issues in Egypt than in most other Arab countries. Egyptian scholars and journalists have written extensively about the various Arab-Israeli wars. And while the Egyptian government has not opened its archives generally, several high level Egyptian officials have had access to them or have revealed information about high-level decision-making to an extent that rarely occurs in the Arab world. Mohammed Heikal's several books on Egyptian foreign relations, based on his own personal access to Nasser and other high-level officials, are especially well known.

But while Egyptians have written much about their wars with Israel and their relations with the superpowers, I could find very little Egyptian literature about Nasser's intervention in Yemen. Maybe this work just hadn't been translated into English, I thought. So while in Cairo, I hoped to interview Egyptian officials and scholars about Cairo's complicated involvement in the Yemeni civil war.

I found that scholars and officials in Egypt were eager to talk about the various Arab-Israeli wars, about which they seemed to have memorized what had happened in enormous detail, and Egypt's relations with both Moscow and Washington at great length. But they seemed strangely reluctant to talk about Yemen.

Whenever I would bring the subject up, my Egyptian interlocutors would ignore me and talk about something else. When I would press them about it, they would respond that they didn't really know much about Yemen; it wasn't their specialty.

I would ask, "Then who is a specialist on Yemen here in Egypt?"

Most people said they did not know. Once, though, I was told, "Well, there is someone who wrote a dissertation on this subject at Cairo University."

"How can I contact him?"

"It isn't easy. He doesn't really have a job. And he doesn't have a phone at home. But if I see him, I'll tell him to contact you."

I never heard from him.

I did, however, meet with Ismail Fahmy, the former Egyptian foreign minister. I interviewed him at his elegant apartment in the exclusive Zamalyk section of Cairo.

Just as in every other interview, I could not get Fahmy to say anything about Yemen, though he was quite voluble about the Arab-Israeli conflict as well as the superpowers. I finally grew exasperated and demanded to know why neither he nor anyone else would talk with me about Yemen. Egyptian forces had fought there for five years. Nasser had called it Egypt's Vietnam. Surely the experience in Yemen equaled the Arab-Israeli conflict as something significant for Egyptian foreign policy specialists to reflect upon.

Fahmy seemed a little taken aback by this outburst. "Oh yes," he said, "the Yemeni civil war is definitely worthwhile for us to think about. The Yemenis defeated us, just like the Israelis did. But the defeats were very different from each other.

"We feel no shame at being defeated by the Israelis," he continued. "Israel, after all, was strongly backed by America and the West. The USSR did not help us nearly as much as America helped Israel. We could hardly be expected to prevail against Israel. Just having fought them at all when the odds were so heavily against us makes us feel heroic.

"But Yemen was different. This was a nation of primitive tribesmen. There was no American support for the royalists. The Soviets gave lots of help to us. We should have won that war, but we lost it. And the fact that the republicans who were about to be defeated when we left then went on to win afterward just adds insult to injury.

"We thought it would be so simple when we first went there. But it is a very complicated country. We never understood it.

"Now do you see why we don't like to talk about it?"

* * *

While I was in town, the American University in Cairo (AUC) arranged a lunch for my wife and me, and for me to give a seminar afterward.

At the lunch, the professors told us something about AUC. It was not like its much larger sister institution--the American University in Beirut. The

AUB had been the center of much of the Arab world's intellectual ferment. The AUC, by contrast, was more of a finishing school for girls from wealthy Arab families. Seventy-five percent of the AUC student body was female--a very unusual ratio for an institution of higher education in the Muslim world. The professors complained that many of their students were less interested in academic pursuits than social ones. But this, I would learn several years later when I became a professor, was hardly unique to AUC students.

Four professors had taken my wife and me to lunch at a restaurant near the university. When we got back to the campus, two of them volunteered to show us around while the other two attended to some business before the start of the seminar. The campus seemed like an oasis of wealth and luxury in the sea of poverty that is Cairo.

We walked by the courts where young Arab women in short skirts were vigorously playing tennis. We observed several groups of students talking casually with one another or with their professors. An enthusiastic, happy outlook seemed to pervade the entire campus.

As the time for the seminar approached, we entered the building where it would be held. Half way down the corridor, we passed by a handsome young Arab man and an attractive young Arab woman walking hand in hand. They were obviously very much in love, and made a very pleasant sight.

There was a good sized audience in the seminar room when we got there. We waited a few minutes for the other two professors we had had lunch with to arrive. But when they didn't show up, the professor introducing me thought we had better get started before we lost the audience we had.

About half way through the presentation, the two finally came in. They sat at the back of the room. It appeared to me that they were angry about something. After the seminar was over, we found out why.

"Did you happen to see a young Arab couple holding hands in the corridor?" asked one.

We responded affirmatively. "Well you weren't the only ones who did," he continued. "There was a Saudi prince here who came to see about getting his daughter admitted. We were walking with him when he saw them."

"What happened?" I asked.

"'How can you permit such a thing?' the prince asked.

"We told him that it was not the role of the university to prevent students from holding hands.

"The prince became extremely upset. 'If my daughter enrolls here as a student, what guarantee can you provide me that she will remain a virgin?'

"We told him that the university could provide no such guarantee; only his daughter could.

"'Then I don't care how badly she wants to be a student here,' said the prince. 'I will never allow her to attend such a school!' He turned around and left right then and there.

"These Saudi princes," the professor concluded, "all have highly unrealistic expectations about what the university can do to chaperone their daughters."

"Or maybe," said my wife, "they have a highly realistic idea about how their daughters will behave if the university doesn't chaperone them."

* * *

Our friend Ahmed was part owner of a travel agency in Cairo. He was in Washington when we told him that we would soon visit Egypt and that we had booked passage on the Nile Hilton's tour boat for a cruise along the river to Luxor and Aswan.

"Why pay so much money?" Ahmed chided us. "I can get you the same tour for far less." Ahmed's argument persuaded us. We agreed to take his tour, and so we canceled our booking for the Hilton's.

When it came time for our boat trip, Ahmed took us to the Cairo train station himself and installed us in our private sleeper in the French-built train that would take us overnight to Luxor where the boat was. We were especially grateful for this service since we doubted we could have negotiated the utter chaos and confusion of the station by ourselves.

Our sleeper was comfortable. The dinner was very good. The service was solicitous. If the train tracks we were traveling over had not been in such poor repair, I might have slept. As it was, the train rattled continuously through the night. It always seemed to jerk especially violently just as I was about to nod off.

The train pulled in at Luxor as dawn was breaking. But Ahmed's agent was right there to take us and our belongings to the boat. As we drove through Luxor, the first call to prayer sounded majestically throughout the city.

We arrived bleary-eyed at our boat, the *King Mina*, just as the last of the passengers from the previous cruise were disembarking. (A cruise on the *King Mina* lasted four nights, beginning in Luxor and ending at Aswan, or vice versa). We checked in and were shown to our cabin on the bottom deck. We were so exhausted that we went straight to sleep. When we woke up several hours later, we realized that things weren't quite right. The cabin stunk. We soon discovered why: the toilet didn't work.

We quickly went upstairs to the desk to ask for a new cabin. After an annoying amount of hesitation on the part of the clerk there, the manager agreed to move us to another one on a higher deck. Everything was moved efficiently. Our new cabin did not smell as bad as the first one. The toilet in it worked, though the shower did not. We suspected there would be no point in asking for yet another cabin; this was probably as good as it was going to get. After talking with our fellow passengers later, we learned that our suspicions were justified.

All the passengers gathered in the dining room for lunch, our first meal of the cruise. The dining room looked like it could hold over a hundred people. There were only ten of us. The staff looked forlorn, except for the maitre d' who greeted us all with an unctuous solicitude.

The ten of us rapidly introduced ourselves to one another. Besides my wife and I, there was an elderly couple from England, a younger English couple who lived in Hong Kong, an elderly French doctor and his voluble wife, a younger single Frenchman who was also a doctor, and a single woman in her early twenties from Canada.

Perhaps our small number depressed the cook. The lunch he served us, at any rate, was uninspiring. Most of us just sort of picked at it. When it was clear that we had finished eating, the waiters came and took our plates away. "I hope you enjoyed your lunch," said the maitre d' with an oily enthusiasm. We all mumbled in response and hoped that dinner would be better.

It wasn't. In fact, dinner looked an awful lot like what we had left on our plates at lunch. There was also something that looked like eggplant. My wife and four others decided to eat what was given to them; it was better than nothing, they said. The remaining passengers and I weren't so sure, and so we just picked at our meal again, despite our hunger.

A funny thing happened later that night. Everyone who had eaten the eggplant became violently ill. I telephoned the ship's officer to complain about the poor food and how it had affected my wife and some of the others. I was connected to the maitre d'. Something in his tone of voice told me that he had heard this complaint before; he didn't seem at all surprised by it.

"It could not have been *our* food," he assured me. "Perhaps they ate something bad before coming to the boat."

Apparently several others had complained as well, because the next morning when we were all seated at breakfast, the maitre d' said, in what he undoubtedly thought was a jovial tone of voice, "Sometimes Westerners are not accustomed to Egyptian food at first. But they get used to it eventually."

The message to us was clear: as far as he was concerned, if the food on the boat made us ill, it was obviously our own fault. He and the rest of the dining room staff, though, looked increasingly discomfited as we passengers took to bringing our own crackers, fruit, candy, and anything else edible to this and every subsequent meal. Still, they were not sufficiently discomfited to significantly alter the menu until dinner on the fourth and final night of the cruise.

* * *

Actually, the term "cruise" was something of a misnomer, at least at first, since the boat didn't budge from its dock at Luxor until the morning of the tour's third day.

But we were not idle during this period. A tour guide took us all around the area. We saw the Valley of the Kings, the Valley of the Queens, and various other monuments.

All were stunning--even overwhelming. Ancient Egypt's obsession with death was unappealing to us. But we couldn't help marveling at the magnificence of what had been built so long ago with primitive technology.

Ancient Egypt's past seemed especially magnificent in contrast to modern Egypt's squalidness, which constantly pressed around us. Wherever we went, beggars would appear. And Egyptian beggars are not only aggressive and persistent, but finicky.

Some beggars absolutely refused to accept Egyptian money. If I offered it to them, they would indicate extreme distaste. "American dollar!" they would shout. But even then, they did not want worn bills; only crisp new bills would satisfy them. "Beggars can't be choosers" was obviously not their philosophy.

They also seemed to possess a remarkable degree of familiarity with American immigration law. "You sponsor me to America!" we often heard, more as a command than a request.

Our guide in Luxor was a little more subtle--or at least he thought he was. Like the boat crew, he could not hide his dismay that there were so few passengers when he first came to collect us. He told us all that he had wanted to become an Egyptologist. He had studied this subject diligently at Cairo University, but alas (he actually said "alas") was unable to find a job that paid a decent salary in his field. So he decided to become a tour guide in upper Egypt in order to be near and explain to others the monuments he loved so dearly.

A couple of times, he talked with my wife and I privately while we were riding in the tour bus that carted us around. He told us how he was engaged to be married, but he and his fiancee had to postpone the wedding until they somehow had enough money to set up their own household. They also had dreams of going to America and studying Egyptology there. "I really depend on the generous tips that foreign visitors give me," he added. "It's really bad when the tour groups are small like this one."

We noticed that he made a point of talking privately with the other couples on the tour also. And he spent a lot of time talking to the Canadian woman, Karen. We assumed that he was telling them all the same story about how he and his fiancee were unable to marry due to lack of money. Obviously, he hoped to increase his tip. His actions also made it clear to those who might not know better--such as myself--that a tip was expected.

Unfortunately for the tour guide, we all began to compare notes as to what he had told us. The story differed somewhat in each case. He told the three from France that his fiancee was finishing medical school and hoped to do her residency in Paris. The English couples were told that both he and she were interested in business and hoped to study that subject in London. But he made no mention of a fiancee to Karen. Instead, he told her how beautiful she was and how he had fallen in love with her. If he and Karen became engaged, she could obtain the Canadian equivalent of a green card for him. In the meantime, he made several suggestions as to how the two of them might become better acquainted in the all too short period of time that fate had thrown them together at present.

Needless to say, he didn't get much by way of tips from any of us. And what we did give was all in soiled Egyptian currency. As he waved goodbye to us from the dock at Luxor when our boat pulled out, he looked genuinely confused.

Karen acquired another admirer in Luxor. Before dinner on the second evening, she went jogging in her T-shirt and shorts. As she came back toward the boat, we observed a young boy on a bicycle riding beside her. He looked like he was eleven or twelve to us. He was saying something and she was laughing. Then she came on board the boat and the boy rode away.

"What did that boy say that made you laugh?" my wife asked when she came up to us.

Karen burst out laughing again. "`Just five minutes!' he told me. `That's all I need with you! Just five minutes!' It was definitely the direct approach."

* * *

Once we began cruising, our spirits picked up considerably. Observing life along the banks of the Nile was fascinating. In some places, the land was lush with vegetation and was intensively cultivated. In others, the desert came right to the water's edge. The sky changed from blue to a magnificent orange at sunset.

We stopped to visit temples at Edfu and Esne. A new, Aswan-based guide awaited us. He was older and more dignified than the previous guide. He also had a far deeper knowledge and appreciation for what he was showing us. The trio from France loved him because he spoke French as well as English. Nor did he ever ask for or make hints about a tip.

At nightfall, our boat docked near the temple of Komombo, though it was too dark to see it then. When we woke up the next morning and looked outside, we saw that we were not alone. Two other tour boats--both larger than ours--were also in the vicinity. The bigger of the two, we were told, belonged to the Nile Hilton.

All of us on the *King Mina* looked at it with envy. We could see several dozen passengers on its deck. Waiters in tuxedos appeared to be serving them their morning champagne. We were seething with envy, especially since we knew what a miserable breakfast awaited us on our boat.

Sooner than we were ready, our new guide came aboard and insisted that we had to go visit the temple immediately. We were a bit surprised at his sense of urgency. But off we went.

The temple was certainly well worth seeing. There were hieroglyphics everywhere. The French doctors were especially pleased when our guide pointed out a set which depicted ancient Egyptian medical instruments. Many of them, the doctors declared, were similar to ones which were still used today, or had been only recently replaced with high technology equivalents.

After walking around for nearly an hour, our guide insisted that we return to the boat immediately. We surmised that there must be a busy itinerary for today. The other two boats, though, were clearly not on such a tight schedule since their passengers had only recently disembarked to see the temple as we were reembarking. But literally just before we got on board the *King Mina,* an enormous wind blew up. The sky instantly turned brown as dirt and dust swirled all around us. We dashed behind the protective safety of a covered-in deck. From there we could make out the passengers from the two other boats scrambling back to their vessels in the dust.

With pride in his voice, our guide told us, "This time of year, the wind comes up strong almost every morning here at Komombo. I don't know why other guides don't plan for it."

We all felt triumphant that in this one instance, the *King Mina's* passengers had been better served than the Hilton's.

* * *

After the wind died down about a half an hour later, our boat's engines were started and we continued our journey to Aswan. I had had high expectations about how exotic Luxor would be--none of which were met. In fact, it was ugly and dirty. I expected more of the same in Aswan. But Aswan turned out to be an attractive, pleasant city. An even greater surprise was that it was clean.

Our guide took us by bus to the old Aswan Dam built by the British during their heyday here. We also visited the enormous High Dam that the Soviets built later. Afterward, we went back to the river where we boarded a *fellucca*--an approximately fifteen foot long boat with an enormous sail. The crew consisted of one young Nubian man who expertly guided the *fellucca* with the sail alone; there was no rudder.

We visited some gardens, a mosque, and a few other places. As the sun was setting, the sky turned a brilliant orange. The evening light played on the sails of other *felluccas* and made beautiful patterns on the water. It was wonderful. The earlier unpleasantness of the trip seemed a dim memory.

When we got back to the *King Mina*, our Aswan guide said good-bye. We had agreed in advance that he deserved a generous tip from each of us--and in hard currency too. He seemed slightly embarrassed at this.

We thought we would be brought back to harsh reality at dinner, but the dining room staff went out of its way to please us on this fourth and last night. Dinner was very good! But it did not appear that a desire to please or a guilty conscience had belatedly affected our hosts. By each place setting was an envelope marked "TIPS" in bold letters. We all gave, but only in Egyptian currency.

As we checked out after breakfast the next morning, we were invited to write our comments about the trip in a special log book that the manager presented to us. I flipped through it. On virtually every page, there were comments such as: "This is the worst boat ride I've ever taken," "The next time there's a war with Israel, I hope the *King Mina* crew is put on the front lines," and "We want our money back!" It was obvious that none of the ship's crew had ever bothered to read the log, for they certainly wouldn't want anyone to see it if they had.

Since our train did not leave until about 2:30 p.m., the manager agreed to store our luggage for us while we toured Aswan on our own. My wife and I walked around with the elderly English couple; it was very relaxing. When we came back to the boat for our luggage, a huge group of Italians had already checked in. The staff was notably happier. Just as our luggage was being taken off the boat, two young Italian women were telling the clerk at the front desk that something was wrong with their cabin and they wanted to change. My wife and I thought we knew which cabin they were talking about.

Outside, Ahmed's man in Aswan was waiting for us. He took us to the train station's cafe where he bought us tea. As Ahmed had before, he installed us in our sleeping compartment when the train was ready for boarding. The train departed Aswan at 2:40 p.m. Sixteen hours, twenty-six minutes, and seventeen seconds later, we pulled into Cairo, just in time for the morning rush hour.

* * *

Life in Cairo is frenetic. There are too many people. Nothing seems to work. Poverty is everywhere. Everything appears on the verge of collapse. Life there seems impossible. Yet somehow it goes on.

The Egyptians say that the main problem with Cairo is that it was built to accommodate two million people, but over twelve million actually live there. Of those twelve million, it seemed to me, fully three million are riding around in cars, trucks, or buses at any one time. "Seeing is believing" is a common phrase. But I could not believe that the horrendous Cairo traffic was reality and not a bad dream when I first saw it.

What makes it so bad? There are three reasons. First, there is the sheer volume of vehicles. I was astounded that a country which was so poor could have so many. But most of them, I observed, were fairly dilapidated. Cairo has a way of ageing cars quickly, my Egyptian friends told me.

Second, this immense volume of vehicles appears to move at only two speeds: either at a crawl, or at over seventy miles per hour. What is more, the traffic shifts back and forth between these two speeds several times a minute.

Third, there don't appear to be any traffic rules. Well, there probably are rules. But no one seems to obey them. Indeed, people make up their own as they go along. The result is that traffic is far more fluid in Cairo than in the more staid West. Cars weave in and out constantly--which is quite a feat when the usual distance between them appears to be no more than a yard, even at high speed.

As a result, being in a car in Cairo can be terrifying. When we were driving with Ahmed, he was constantly lurching forward and screeching to a halt while simultaneously weaving in and out, like everyone else. We were surrounded by a continuous symphony of honking horns and shouting drivers. Our friend did his share of shouting and honking too after each near miss with another vehicle--a process that seemed to occur literally every few seconds.

Once my wife and I had a whispered conversation in the back seat over whether we should ask our friend to please drive more carefully. We decided against it because it was clear that driving in Cairo demanded our friend's full attention; distracting him with a call to drive more slowly might cause the accident we hoped to avoid.

But if Cairo traffic looks frightening from inside a car, it is much worse from the standpoint of a pedestrian. There does not appear to be any concept of "pedestrian right of way" in Cairo. In order to cross a street, then, a pedestrian has to make a mad dash from one side to the other in the midst of oncoming traffic. Crossing at corners where there are traffic lights is not easier than anywhere else since there are always an immense number of cars turning right or left in front of where the pedestrian must cross.

Cairo drivers appear to have no sympathy for pedestrians. They don't slow down at all for them or anyone else. Once while we were walking along the Corniche, my wife and I saw a truck hit a bicycle. The bike fell over and the cyclist fell on the road hard. The truck came to a stop and the two men riding in it got out. I assumed they would help the cyclist up, but as soon as they reached him, they began to kick him repeatedly--apparently for getting in their way. The cyclist rapidly got up, remounted his now wobbly bicycle, and pedaled off as best he could amidst the continuing curses of the two truckers. A Kenyan woman witnessing this with us shook her head in disbelief. "These Egyptians are crazy!" she declared.

Besides crossing the street, pedestrians face another problem. Although there are crumbling sidewalks in much of Cairo, the pedestrian often cannot use them but must walk in the street instead. This is because drivers park their cars on the sidewalks--which, of course, is why the sidewalks are crumbling.

Due to the great volume of cars and people on both the sidewalks and the streets, walking outside takes tremendous concentration and can be very tiring. One day we walked around outside for an especially long period of time sightseeing. We were so exhausted when we came back to our apartment that we spent the entire next day inside; we just couldn't face Cairo again so soon.

* * *

But even staying inside an apartment building does not allow you to escape from Cairo's peculiarities. The elevator in our building was tiny; my wife and I could barely fit in it together. But at least it worked, after a fashion.

Egyptian Interlude

We never knew when we opened the door to get in or out whether the elevator floor would be above or below the floor of the landing--sometimes by as much as two feet. I think the two were on the same level only once; something must have been wrong.

All other elevators in Cairo seemed to work on the same principle--if they worked at all. At least the light worked in ours. In many they didn't, which presented a real challenge in the dark because of the uneven floors problem.

A lot of elevators didn't work at all--nor did they ever seem to be repaired. This meant you had to use the stairwell, which was never lit.

But while dark elevators or stairwells were a problem for us, they didn't seem to phase most Cairenes. Their eyes appear to have undergone additional evolution allowing them to adjust from broad daylight outside to pitch black inside without any transition. Our Egyptian friends assured us that we would develop this ability in time also--if we could only avoid breaking our necks in the meantime.

One other standard feature of apartment buildings in Cairo is that no matter how expensive and luxuriant the apartments themselves may be (and many are), there is always a mountain of dirt on each floor outside the apartments themselves. These were usually explained as repairs. But like the Pyramids, they never disappeared. Children used them as indoor sandlots.

Yet another maddening feature of life in Cairo is the telephone system. Just making a local phone call takes extraordinary persistence. First, there is the problem of getting a dial tone. This can take several tries. Then, there is the problem of dialing. Often, as soon as you dial the first or second digit of the phone number, a busy signal will sound. Even if you succeed in dialing the entire number, nothing at all may happen. It feels like triumph when you finally hear the phone at the other end ring. But surprisingly often, the system connects you with a completely different number from the one you dialed. And if you experience any one of these problems, you must, of course, start all over again from which point you may well run into some or all of these problems over and over and over again.

When you finally do get hold of the person you want, there are still problems. Often, you can barely hear the person on the other end of the line. The Egyptians claim this is the result of the primitive bugging system installed by Soviet "experts" back when Cairo and Moscow were closely allied. It's especially hard to hear the other person when you also hear his or her phone still ringing even though the phone has been answered.

Receiving phone calls can also be a problem. Often, I would see people who said they tried to call me for hours the previous evening. But while we may have been home the entire time, we never heard the phone ring. Or sometimes it would ring, but the line would be dead when I answered it. Or sometimes, someone would call and the problem of hearing them would be aggravated by my phone continuing to ring loudly. Yet we dare not hang up and try again for fear of being unable to re-establish the connection for hours.

Another maddening aspect of receiving phone calls has less to do with the poor phone system and more to do with a quirk of the Egyptians. When Egyptians call, they never identify themselves. They always want to see if you recognize their voice. In Cairo, though, I found it difficult to recognize anyone's voice when I could barely hear it on a poor quality connection.

I must say, though, virtually all Egyptians I have telephoned have recognized my voice instantly--even if they have only spoken to me once before years ago. Perhaps, like being able to see in pitch dark, recognizing voices instantly is another example of additional evolution experienced by Egyptians as a result of having to live with chronically poor telephone lines.

* * *

The problems we had to cope with, though, were nothing compared to the problems of poor Cairenes. The poverty in Cairo is of a different magnitude altogether than the poverty that exists in the West. Everywhere you can see large numbers of people who are clearly undernourished roaming the streets. Many appear to be suffering from various illnesses, but are obviously not receiving any form of medical attention. You can see poverty on a vast scale in the City of the Dead--the enormous grave yard where thousands of poor people have taken up residence. And wherever a Westerner appears, an army of piteous looking beggars will quickly be mustered.

Although Cairo's poverty seems bad from inside a car, it appears much worse when you are on foot. My wife and I got an especially "up close and personal" view of this poverty the day we decided to walk from our apartment in Garden City to the Coptic Cathedral (about twenty percent of the Egyptian population is Coptic Christian).

Like typical Americans, we planned our trip by looking at a map and plotting our course along the most direct route between our apartment and the cathedral. Our Egyptian friends told us later that no Cairene would ever do such a thing.

As we walked along the street leading to the cathedral, which we could see in front of us in the distance, we moved deeper and deeper into an immense slum. At the heart of it, an open sewer line ran through the center of the street. There were piles of refuse everywhere--it was impossible to avoid stepping in some of it. The stench was terrifying. And, of course, there were people--thousands and thousands of them, it seemed to us. The filthier ones, we surmised, lived in the street with all the chickens and even cows which we saw there.

We were like magnets to them. They all appeared drawn toward us, many of them begging for money. My wife and I felt a number of feelings simultaneously: pity at the sight of them, nausea from the smell, and the desire to move along as quickly as possible. We did not, however, feel afraid. Despite the fact that we were vulnerable and probably had more money in our pockets than most of them would see in a year, they were friendly.

This was one aspect of Cairo that never ceased to amaze us. Although we had to be wary of all the cars, we felt relatively secure from crime no matter where we walked in Cairo--even at night. We never felt as secure in any major American city as we did in Cairo. While crime certainly exists in Cairo, it does not seem to exist on anywhere near the same scale as it does in the U.S. Despite the fact that some Muslim revolutionaries have begun attacking foreigners in Egypt recently, I think that there is much less prospect for Americans becoming the victim of violence in Cairo than in our own country. The sheer volume of people makes it very difficult for criminal acts to go undetected, or for criminals to flee very far very fast.

Perhaps this is yet another example of difficult conditions in Cairo leading to further evolution among its citizens. Because so many people live in such a small area, a greater degree of civility is absolutely essential just to survive. It is hard to imagine, though, that doubling the population of New York City would lead the people there to become kinder and gentler.

* * *

The question for the future is whether Cairo--and all of Egypt--will remain civil. Many observers say no. They see immense poverty combined with an unresponsive, inefficient, and corrupt government along with an overly-regulated private sector as a recipe for revolution. There have been food riots periodically. The rise of intolerant Muslim revolutionary groups in Egypt, as well as elsewhere in the Middle East, is seen as an ominous sign that change for the worse is on the way.

It might happen. But I'm inclined to think it might not. For the people of Cairo possess something very important to help them cope with life under very difficult circumstances: their extraordinary sense of humor.

It is, however, very difficult to describe. Giving examples can't convey it well either since gestures, tone of voice, and most importantly, a presumed shared familiarity with Cairo life are all essential ingredients. What Cairo humor reveals is a never-ending astonishment that life in Cairo can be so absurd as well as the conviction that attempting to change it would be futile. This is not a sentiment that appears to be highly developed in other Arab countries or in Israel. Perhaps this is because life is controllable to a greater degree, either by the people or by the government, in these other countries. Egyptians, by contrast, know that no one is really in control in Cairo.

And unlike neighboring countries where there is an enormous gulf either between different ethnic groups or between the rulers and the ruled, the very absurdity of life in Cairo actually serves as a unifying force. For everyone in Cairo--whether rich or poor, ruler or ruled--is a victim of the horrendous traffic and the crumbling infrastructure. In Cairo, every encounter with the bureaucracy, every outing to shop, every attempt to get something repaired, even every attempt to make a phone call becomes an extraordinary, heroic adventure and the subject of a story to be recounted later with family and friends. And as much as they complain about and ridicule it, Cairenes love their city fiercely. A Cairene outside of Cairo for very long is often a very sad individual: life anywhere else seems boring. Perhaps more importantly, since life in other cities is easier, the same strong sense of community does not develop that the daily difficulty of surviving in Cairo fosters.

Thus, despite all signs of its imminent collapse, life in Cairo not only continues, but thrives. This paradox may be impossible to comprehend rationally. But Cairenes know that their city cannot be understood rationally, for the simple reason that it is irrational.

Yemen on My Mind

Making arrangements to visit North Yemen back in 1982 was extremely frustrating. It came as no surprise that the North Yemeni embassy in Washington was not in the business of setting up appointments for visiting scholars. Just finding Yemenis in Washington, or anyone who knew any Yemenis, was difficult. Of the few Yemenis I did meet, very few spoke much English. And those who knew English were usually not willing to talk with me after they learned I was studying Soviet relations with their country. Either they wouldn't talk at all, or they would talk about the subject a little bit once but would later not return phone calls or keep appointments.

The staff at the North Yemeni embassy was extremely suspicious of me even before I told them why I wanted to visit North Yemen. I had the impression that Yemeni diplomats didn't have much contact with Americans, but lived in a little world of their own. I didn't know how I was going to get them to give me a visa.

I also contacted a number of current and former U.S. Foreign Service officers who had served in Yemen. Each related a number of anecdotes to me, but indicated that they very much doubted Yemenis would agree to talk to me. My subject of research was too sensitive. One of them put me in touch with the sole American academic group that worked in Yemen--the American Institute for Yemeni Studies--which maintained a hostel in Sanaa, the North Yemeni capital, for visiting scholars. I called up the American-based president of the organization. He was very friendly, but told me quite bluntly that the institute would prefer not to be associated with me for fear that the government might become annoyed at my activities--something he implied was highly likely.

All this was very discouraging. It was now the end of October and I was scheduled to depart for the Middle East on December 1. I didn't want to postpone the trip in order to have more time to make arrangements for Yemen. I had already made detailed plans for both Oman and Egypt which would be too difficult to rearrange. Nor was I confident that any extra time spent attempting to make contacts for my Yemen visit would be productive. I thought I might have to cancel the visit to North Yemen altogether since it would be pointless to go there with absolutely no plans or appointments.

But on Halloween night--the night before I was going to cancel the Yemeni portion of the trip--I received a phone call from a Yemeni graduate student whom I had met. The call came at midnight--the time, I would learn from experience, that Yemenis like best for making telephone calls. In my sleepy state, I understood him to say that a famous Yemeni politician, Shaykh Sinan Abu Lahoum, was currently in Washington. He was staying at the Watergate and I should call him there.

The next day, I wasn't sure whether the phone call I had received was real or a dream. I was inclined to think it was the latter as no Yemeni had been at all helpful to me before this. I thought I should go ahead and call the travel agent to change my ticket; since I was going to Oman first and then Egypt, I would save a lot of money if I came straight home from Cairo instead of backtracking to Yemen. But curiosity got the better of me. I had never met a shaykh before. Although I didn't know why, it struck me as funny that one should stay at the Watergate. So I called the hotel.

The hotel operator put me through to the room. The phone was answered by a woman who did not speak English at all. In my broken Arabic, I left a message. I gave her my phone number in Arabic and spelled my name out for her in Arabic letters (Kaf, alaf, taa, zein--Katz). All this took an inordinate amount of time; the lady, of course, recognized the letters, but couldn't seem to believe that it actually spelled my name. I also had to repeat the phone number several times since she interrupted me by bursting out laughing on several occasions. I guess she thought my accent was funny. When the conversation ended, I strongly doubted that the shaykh would ever see my message or would be able to interpret it if he did.

Two hours later I got a call from a young man who introduced himself as Mohammed Ali Abu Lahoum, a nephew of the shaykh. His English was completely fluent. He asked me what it was I had called for. I told him about my project and how I wanted to interview his uncle. He said he would get back to me. Based on my previous experience, I did not expect to hear from him, but half an hour later Mohammed called to say that the shaykh could see me that very night at the Watergate. And since his uncle did not know English, Mohammed would be there to translate.

That night, I walked from my apartment near Scott Circle down to the

Watergate. In addition to Sinan and Mohammed, Dirham Abu Lahoum was also present. From several calls I had made beforehand, I had learned that Sinan was one of the most colorful figures in Yemeni politics. He was one of the leading shaykhs of the Bakil--one of the two large North Yemeni tribal confederations. Although conservative and religious, he had fought on the side of the republicans during the civil war in the 1960s. He had been governor of Hodeida, the North Yemeni port city, during the siege of Sanaa-- the most fateful event of that particular war. His brother, Dirham, had been governor of Ibb, then of Taiz--two important North Yemeni cities. Both had been members of the ruling presidential council in the early 1970s. But they lost these positions at the time of the 1974 coup which brought the military and the Hashid tribal confederation to power. Shaykh Sinan, however, remained--indeed, still remains--an important politician due to his prominence among the Bakil.

At the Watergate, I learned that Mohammed was a graduate student at nearby George Washington University and--I was especially pleased to discover--worked part time at the North Yemeni embassy. He would later become an important politician in his own right through serving as an elected member in the parliament of first North Yemen, and later, united Yemen. He would also become secretary-general of the Bakil confederation.

It just so happened that the first question I posed to Shaykh Sinan was on a subject close to his heart: the siege of Sanaa. He related to me all the important events of the seventy-two day siege which began on November 28, 1967 when the royalists surrounded Sanaa and the republican cause seemed doomed. But the republicans were able to break the siege. With great pride, he told me about his own role in this defining event from his position as governor of Hodeida.

The three of them also answered all my questions about Soviet-North Yemeni relations in great detail. They displayed none of the suspiciousness or nervousness that other Yemenis did when I asked them about this subject. At the end of the conversation, they offered their family's help in assisting me while in Sanaa. Mohammed--who would become a lifelong friend--said that he would take care of my visa. I decided to go after all.

* * *

After nearly four weeks traveling in Oman and Egypt, my wife and I flew wearily from Cairo to Sanaa on December 29. The flight itself did not bode well for the visit. The Yemenia airliner was two hours late coming into Cairo. On boarding the aircraft, we discovered that Yemenis apparently do not believe in the concept of a line. Everyone--including the women--attempted to charge up the stairwell into the aircraft simultaneously. Nor did they accept the notion of assigned seating; everyone dashed into the nearest seat at hand. As a result, there was no separation between smoking and non-smoking. And everyone around us smoked non-stop throughout the two hour flight.

Before leaving Washington, I had also notified the U.S. embassy in Sanaa that I would be coming. The ambassador himself wrote back saying that he would be glad to see me. When we arrived in Sanaa that evening, we were pleasantly surprised to discover that the political officer--the number three man--had come out to pick us up and drive us to our hotel. It has often been my experience that the smaller the U.S. embassy is, the more readily it will welcome and make much of visiting Americans who write about that particular country. We had experienced this in Oman and were about to experience it again in North Yemen. By contrast, the larger embassies will do almost nothing, as we had recently discovered in Egypt.

There were no lights outside the terminal building and we made our way in almost pitch blackness. There was apparently construction taking place during the day. At one point we had to haul our luggage over two narrow planks placed across a ditch. The hefty man behind us fell off, his suitcase spilling its contents into the night. Welcome to Yemen.

The vehicle we were taken to was a land rover. The political officer explained that this was especially useful for traveling on Yemen's difficult roads outside the capital. Right now, though, even land rovers couldn't get through to many places since there had recently been a major earthquake which had done significant damage to the country's infrastructure. We then proceeded downtown to the Taj Sheeba Hotel--part of the Taj chain based in Bombay.

* * *

The next morning, we awoke to a spectacular view of the Sanaa skyline. Unlike the other countries of the Arabian Peninsula, North Yemen is mountainous. But more spectacular than the view of the hills was Sanaa's architecture. The Yemenis claim that they built the first skyscrapers. Many of their old buildings are several stories tall and made out of stone. Beautiful filigree patterns are carved into their fronts. Above each normal rectangular window is usually another window made of colored glass in the shape of a semi-circle or some other pattern. North Yemen is one of the few Third World countries not to have experienced West European colonialism.

Perhaps as a result of this, its traditional architecture has been replaced by modern Western buildings to a much lesser extent than in other Third World countries.

* * *

The morning after we arrived, the phone rang in our hotel room. I picked up the receiver and said hello. Without introducing himself, the voice on the other end of the line stated, "My mother told me to invite you for lunch today. I will come pick you up in an hour."

It was Adnan, the youngest son of Shaykh Sinan. His invitation was somewhat peremptory, but it was most welcome.

We went down to the hotel lobby at the appointed time. Adnan was half an hour late. He blamed the narrow streets of Sanaa, the capital, which had not been designed for heavy automobile traffic.

"My mother thought you might be lonely just by yourselves in the hotel," Adnan said as we were driving along. "That's why she made me invite you for lunch." He seemed eager to assure us that the invitation was not his idea or something he would have ever thought of on his own.

Adnan informed us that the family was not eating lunch at his father's place that day, but at the home of his uncle, a former general. His was an old, traditional house. It was at least four stories tall and made of white stone. Intricate designs and patterns had been cut into the face of the building. We entered the house through an antique wooden door and went upstairs one flight on a white stone staircase.

We were shown into a Western-style parlor with chairs and couches. Four men were already there waiting for us; two were in their fifties while the other two, like Adnan, were in their twenties. The older pair were the retired general and his brother, a retired colonel. One of the younger men was an engineer; I forget what the other one was. But besides my wife, there were no women present.

Conversation proceeded a little awkwardly at first. The two older brothers knew no English and my wife and I could not converse in Arabic. The younger men served as translators, but since their command of English was not strong, it was a slow process.

Servants came in with lamb soup, which we drank directly from the bowl. It was thick and flavorful.

After a while, we were ushered into the dining room. The "dining table" was a series of three small tables of uneven height. No two of the chairs were alike. The family was used to eating on the floor, but had made this table up so we would feel comfortable.

After the five Yemeni men, two boys, my wife and I all sat down, there were still two chairs which were empty. The wives of the two younger men had been invited to join us, we were told, "but they are too shy."

Lunch turned out to be an immense feast. There was baked lamb, boiled lamb, lamb pilaf, lamb stew, and more lamb soup. There was also a mountain of traditional Yemeni bread which was eaten with a vegetable stew from a pot we were told was two centuries old. My wife and I were continuously urged to eat more and more, even by people who had stopped eating themselves. We felt we couldn't eat a bite more when dessert arrived: jello with canned fruit cocktail--something my wife and I were definitely not expecting to be served in Yemen.

After lunch, we moved to the *mafraj,* or Yemeni sitting room. Seats without legs lined the base of the four walls. In one of the walls was a traditional Yemeni stained glass window with red, yellow, blue, and green panes. A number of small boys darted in and out of the room to get a glimpse of us.

Conversation again seemed strained. Finally the general asked us if we would like to try *qat,* the leaf which Yemenis chew for its effect as a stimulant. Having heard that *qat* was actually a narcotic, we declined.

The general then said something in Arabic to one of the little boys who immediately ran out of the room. He returned about a minute later with an enormous revolver which he handed to the general. I thought at first that we must have committed an unforgivable *faux pas* in refusing to chew *qat,* but the general was just preparing to go out and chew with his friends. Adnan told us later that most Yemeni men, including himself, would feel naked if they went outside without a pistol. After a short while, the colonel called for his pistol and he left too.

With the two older men gone, the atmosphere of the gathering became much more relaxed. The party also grew larger as four or five little boys now entered and remained inside the *mafraj* with us. With the elders gone, I concluded, they felt emboldened. This group was soon followed by a group of four little girls. I had only caught a glimpse of some of them before as they shyly peeped out at us from behind doors. Now they came in tittering and giggling, wearing Western-style dresses. Finally, the wives of the two younger Yemeni men entered. They came in one at a time, and with far greater seriousness than their daughters. They were wearing long, ankle-length skirts. Both sat by my wife.

The conversation became livlier. The Yemeni women did not say anything, but their husbands talked about them: what they could cook, how many children they had, what their bride price had been, etc. With the revolver scene still in my mind, I decided it would be prudent not to look directly at the two women. My wife told me later that they shook like leaves the entire time.

In the midst of this conversation about domestic affairs, one of the little girls--a ten year old--started speaking in surprisingly good English. "I am not going to get married! I believe in women's liberation!"

The men all laughed at this.

I asked her father at what age did Yemeni girls usually get married.

"Fourteen," he responded.

"That's just four years from now for her," I remarked.

The little girl's eyes grew wide. She ran out of the room.

When the party was over, the two women nodded at us and disappeared before we left the house. Along with the men, all the children came outside to see us off, including the little bride-to-be. After the little boys shook hands with me, she came up and offered me her hand too. But before I could take it in mine, she drew it back and looked fearfully at her older male relatives. But they nodded their heads, so she shook hands with me after all.

We said good-bye to everyone one last time, and Adnan drove us back to our hotel. It was only some time after he dropped us off that my wife and I both realized that we had never met his mother--the person who had invited us to lunch in the first place.

* * *

In addition to this lunch, Adnan took us on four excursions outside the capital.

One place we visited was Wadi Dar--a large, lush valley not far from Sanaa. In the valley is an enormous rock which is several stories tall. On top of the rock sits one of the palaces of the former kings. It is practically a sheer vertical ascent to the palace from three sides of the rock. There is a steep, narrow stairway on the fourth. We were not able to go into the palace because of earthquake damage, but I did go inside it on a subsequent visit. The rooms were not very large; most of the space was taken up by an internal stair case.

We were told that as part of his plan to keep his subjects cowed, King Ahmad had a stuffed lion which he would have put out on the balcony of the palace where it was visible. He also had a gramophone recording of a lion roaring which he would play. The lion would apparently roar and roar. But when the king came out onto the balcony, the roaring would stop. The king would even pat the lion. I don't know if the story is true, but it illustrates the popular Yemeni perception of his personality.

Even now, the North Yemeni tribes are strong in the rural areas and the central government must deal with them very gingerly. My first visit took place before the discovery of oil in 1984 when the tribes were even more powerful. Each time Adnan drove us outside the capital, we would go through an army checkpoint. The central government's writ diminished considerably after this while that of the tribes increased. The purpose of the checkpoints, we were told, was not to prevent anyone from going outside the city, but to make sure that people coming in were not carrying weapons.

Adnan also took us to the *soukh* at Bab al-Yaman in the old section of Sanaa. This was literally a maze of tiny streets with vendors selling all kinds of things. I bought a *jambiya*, the traditional Yemeni dagger that all Yemeni males from, it seemed, the age of five wear on a belt across their middle and which looked like an enormous phallus. Mine was a cheap one--only about one hundred U.S. dollars. Expensive *jambiyas* had a pedigree of famous owners going back centuries and sold for fifty thousand dollars or more.

At my wife's urging, we also went to visit the shop of a goldsmith. The proprietor seemed surprised that we preferred to buy something made in Yemen rather than in Italy; while the former seemed exotic to us, it was the latter which seemed exotic to him. We finally bought a bracelet for about three hundred dollars.

A Yemeni lady in the store who was covered in black watched us. After we bought the bracelet, she asked through Adnan, "Are you only buying the one?" She then showed us the dozen or so gold bracelets on her arm. And she was there to buy more.

Most of the Yemeni women we saw were completely covered in black; their veils covered even their eyes. Adnan told us that all Yemeni women wore black, except the elderly ones. They were allowed to wear robes of equal modesty, but with different colors. If we ever saw a Yemeni woman outside with her hair and face uncovered, this was a sure sign that she was from Aden--the capital of South Yemen--where more liberal customs concerning how women dressed had been adopted under the British.

* * *

The embassy people treated us very nicely too. The political officer had us over to his home on New Year's Eve. One other rule about U.S. embassies: the more difficult the post, the nicer the housing that the embassy staff lives in. He offered us alcohol, which back then could be purchased easily in Sanaa, but was very expensive. A seven ounce can of beer cost about five dollars. He did warn us that the high altitude tended to make the effect of the alcohol more potent.

He then proceeded to tell us his tale of woe. He had come to Sanaa married to a beautiful and brilliant young French woman. She had, however, left him for someone else at the embassy. Now he was bereft. My wife suggested that perhaps he might meet someone else, but he replied that he was very particular. She had to be both brilliant and beautiful. She also had to be French. And Protestant. And eighteen (he was in his late thirties at least). In short, he wanted a new version of his first wife.

We felt very sorry for him. For not only are French Protestants fairly thin on the ground these days, but as a professor I can testify that brilliance is seldom evident in eighteen year olds.

On a more professional note, the ambassador invited me to come talk with him and his staff the day after New Year's. A three year long Marxist insurgency had just been defeated six months previously. I asked a lot about this and the role of the Soviets generally. These issues, however, were not what was preoccupying them at the moment. The tribes were instead. It was all too common, they said, for the tribes to relieve people of their vehicles out in the countryside. A nasty incident had just occurred. A group of tribesmen had blocked the road somewhere and had snared a U.S. embassy land rover. After it had stopped, the tribesmen--who were all heavily armed--surrounded the vehicle and demanded that the two embassy personnel get out. The Americans refused and attempted to drive away. One of the younger tribesmen fired a bullet into one of the front tires to prevent the land rover from moving. But the bullet had ricocheted up through the floor board and lodged in the foot of one of the embassy officers. The other one declared that he couldn't give the tribesmen the land rover now as he needed it to rush his colleague to a hospital. Fortunately, the tribesmen accepted this argument and let them drive off in their land rover. It was this kind of problem--as well as the occasional rocket-launched grenade fired into the embassy compound--that American diplomats had to deal with in Yemen.

* * *

Yemen is not a country that has been written about much in the Western press. It usually only receives coverage when the Yemenis are at war with each other--which, unfortunately, has all too often been the case. But what coverage Yemen received, I discovered, was often misleading. Back when there were two Yemens, the South was always described as "Marxist" while the North was always described as "conservative." The South was indeed Marxist, to an extent. It had all the trappings of a Marxist state, including a Marxist party with a politburo, central committee, secretariat, and military advisers from the USSR, East Germany, and Cuba. But as would be seen during the bloody 1986 civil war between rival factions of the ruling party there, tribal and regional loyalties were more important even to the Marxists than loyalty to each other.

Misunderstanding South Yemen, though, was excusable. The government there allowed very few Westerners into the country, and from what some of those who did get in told me, their visits were very tightly controlled. Misunderstanding North Yemen was, I thought, far less excusable. For despite the reluctance of its diplomats in Washington and elsewhere to talk with foreigners, my friend Mohammed told me that North Yemeni embassies did in fact grant visas to all who requested one. Very few, however, ever did--especially journalists.

But even a very short visit to North Yemen would inform anyone that applying the term "conservative" to it was too simplistic. North Yemen was certainly conservative in terms of social mores, especially for women. But the ideology of the regime could not accurately be described as conservative at all. The "republican" government, after all, was the product of a revolution, and viewed itself as revolutionary. The regime's propaganda was largely anti-American and pro-Soviet. Back then, most of the news that North Yemenis received about America and the West came from TASS--the Soviet news agency. North Yemen also publicly supported all manner of Third World revolutionary causes, especially those in the Middle East. The North Yemeni press seldom offered any criticism of the Soviet Union, even when the vast majority of Third World nations condemned Moscow for the Soviet invasion of Afghanistan.

The Western press's insistence that North Yemen was "conservative" was simply wrong. Perhaps it was something journalists assumed "had to be" logically. If South Yemen was Marxist, and if the North and the South were often at odds with each other, then clearly the North "had to be" conservative. What they did not understand was that ordinary logic did not apply in the case of the Yemens.

* * *

Besides the Abu Lahoums, I was able to make appointments with three other Yemenis. One was an adviser to the foreign minister. I went to his office where I was kept waiting for an hour. When I asked him to characterize North Yemen's relations with its neighbors and the two superpowers, he immediately became highly defensive. He insisted that North Yemen's relations were "excellent" with all of them except, of course, the United States. He then gave me the standard harangue about the evils of American aid to the Zionists. I asked him whether, in addition to its support to Israel, the North Yemenis would like to see the U.S. reduce its support to Saudi Arabia with which North Yemen has often had tense relations. He completely denied that any such tension existed. I reminded him that a South Yemeni-backed insurgency against North Yemen had just ended about six months ago. Surely relations between North and South must still be tense, I suggested. He not only denied that there was any tension between the two, but also that there had been a South Yemeni-backed insurgency against the North.

Becoming annoyed at this line of questioning, the adviser then embarked on another harangue against the U.S. for having provided his country with what he described as only a small amount of relief assistance after the recent earthquake. I reminded him that it was well known that the Soviets had sent far less--next to nothing really. Did he have similarly negative views about the Soviets? He didn't deny that this was true, but instead of criticizing it, he made excuses on Moscow's behalf. "Besides," he insisted, "Soviet assistance is more long term." Shortly after this I thanked him for sharing his insights with me and left. I sincerely hoped that the analysis he supplied to his minister was more sophisticated than that which he provided to me. But somehow I doubted it.

* * *

The second appointment I made was with someone who worked at the Survey Authority--the office which made maps for the North Yemeni government. He was not an obvious person to talk with about the subject I was interested in. I had met him at the North Yemeni embassy in Washington while I was waiting to get my visa. He had recently finished a graduate degree in the USSR and was visiting Washington briefly. He openly acknowledged that the quality of life he saw in Washington, D.C. was far superior to anything in the USSR. He thought, however, that Washington might be something of a Potemkin village which the imperialists had set up to impress foreigners like him. He suspected that the vast army of America's unemployed, which he had heard so much about in the USSR, was being held at bay outside the Beltway.

Since he had urged me to call him when I came to Sanaa, I did so and we made an appointment to meet at his office. Fortunately, the Survey Authority was just a short walk from my hotel. When I arrived, though, it soon became clear that I was not going to learn much more from this individual than I already had in Washington. Half a dozen of his friends--all male, of course--were in his office when I arrived there. They all seemed highly suspicious of me. When I began to ask about Yemeni relations with the USSR, three of them in turn delivered a bitter oration against American support for Israel. It was because of this, I was told, that Arab states, including Yemen, had turned to Moscow. I tried mightily to get them to briefly turn their attention away from America's relations with Israel to the Soviet Union's relations with North Yemen. They admitted that there were "advantages and disadvantages" for North Yemen in their relationship with Moscow. But when I asked them to state specifically what these advantages and disadvantages were, they refused.

The conversation was not a total loss: they did give me a bottle of orange soda and a wall map of Yemen. As I was leaving the grounds of the Survey Authority, however, a large number of men would not let me pass by them through the gate. I found myself surrounded by a shouting crowd. I thought they wanted money, but someone who spoke English said that the map I was carrying did not have the approval stamp needed for it to be taken outside the grounds of the Survey Authority. They thought I might be stealing it. So I went back inside where I spent a long time searching for an approval stamp for a map I really did not want. I would have abandoned the map in the building, but I feared that if I tried to leave the grounds without it, the crowd at the gate would see this as prima facie evidence that I had been trying to steal it. I had to go to several offices before someone finally stamped the map for me. After being carefully inspected by the gang at the gate, I was finally allowed to leave amidst a chorus of salaams.

* * *

The third appointment, which the U.S. embassy arranged for me, was with Dr. `Abd al-Aziz al-Saqqaf. He was a professor of economics at Sanaa University who had received his Ph.D. in the U.S. He was kind enough to invite my wife and me to his home for dinner one evening.

Like the Abu Lahoums, he was not at all reticent to talk about anything. Indeed, our conversation was so open that he and I rapidly discovered that we disagreed on practically everything. The discussion soon deteriorated into a shouting match. What especially infuriated me about him was that he assumed that there was an "American viewpoint" (which, of course, was wrong) on any given subject, and that I shared that viewpoint since I too was American. He was the most stubborn, bullheaded person I had ever met. I, by contrast, was most certainly a paragon of good manners. If I raised my voice at all, it was only out of concern that he might have the benefit of hearing what I had to say even as he was shouting himself.

The experience was so unpleasant that I made no effort to contact Dr. al-Saqqaf on my next three visits to Sanaa. Nor did he ever contact me when he visited Washington, as I heard he had. I had forgotten him altogether when on my fifth visit to Yemen in 1992--a period when a considerable degree of political and press freedom was being allowed--I picked up a copy of the *Yemen Times*. The paper--which was the only English-language weekly published in Sanaa--was remarkably critical of the government, I thought. When I looked at the masthead, I was surprised to discover that the editor and publisher was none other than Dr. al-Saqqaf.

Although we did not meet in person, we had a long--and highly civilized--telephone conversation. I arranged to subscribe to the paper, which I read thoroughly whenever it arrived. In it, Dr. al-Saqqaf regularly criticized and called for the resignation of various cabinet ministers and even the president himself. I came to appreciate that his stubbornness and bullheadedness were virtues, not vices. Indeed, Dr. al-Saqqaf's insistence on speaking out even when the government attempted to intimidate him into not doing so was an act of great courage.

He and I had agreed on one thing that evening in January 1983: the two Yemens, we both predicted, would never ever unite. When they did unite in May 1990, I began to suspect that when two academics agree on something, then they both must be wrong.

* * *

The day before we left, the U.S. embassy's deputy chief of mission and his wife had us over to lunch at their home--which was even bigger than the political officer's and had more servants. We thought it must be hard for Foreign Service officers to return from posts like Sanaa, where the State Department subsidized them in an aristocratic lifestyle, to Washington where they got no special allowance for life in that expensive city. As we were seen off early the next morning at the airport by both the embassy's public affairs officer and Adnan Abu Lahoum, we reflected that life back home was going to seem a little pedestrian to us too after being treated so kindly in Sanaa. As the Air France jet took off, we had a last look at Sanaa bathed in the fiery red light of sunrise, and so began our long journey home.

Saudi Sojourn

I met him at a reception. I told him that I was about to take my first trip to the Middle East, visiting Egypt, Oman, and Yemen. He asked me why I wasn't visiting his country, Saudi Arabia.

I explained that although I am not Jewish, my last name is and therefore I didn't think the Saudis would let me in. He said that this was nonsense. He told me I could be allowed in even if I was Jewish. He also said that he would not only get me a visa for the kingdom, but would arrange for me to meet with several ministers. He could do this, he said, because he himself was a minister's son.

Over the course of the next year and a half, I got to know this young Saudi quite well. Like all other Arabs I have known, he opposed Israeli occupation of Arab territories. But unlike most others, he was interested both in Judaism and in Israel. After I knew him awhile, he admitted that he was actually taking private lessons in Hebrew.

He was also working on a Ph.D. In his program, he had to have two professors approve of his dissertation. He had chosen a prominent Arab scholar as his primary reader, but had also selected a well-known Israeli scholar as the second member of his committee. This was the first time I had ever heard of a Saudi seeking out a Jew to work with on a dissertation, and I was impressed at my friend's broadmindedness.

* * *

After eighteen months had passed, I strongly doubted that my friend could organize a visit to Saudi Arabia for me. But then one day, he phoned and said, "Your visit to the kingdom has been approved. How soon can you come?" We arranged for me to go the very next month.

Except for Muslims making the pilgrimage to the holy cities of Mecca and Medina, gaining entry into Saudi Arabia is not easy. Despite its abundance of sand and sun, the kingdom does not grant tourist visas. All visa applications are scrutinized closely, the Saudi consular officer who gave me my visa said. In fact, he actually had a disincentive to grant visas. For if a visitor to the kingdom broke the law, the government would hold the consular officer who granted his visa personally responsible. The government's theory was that somehow the consular officer "should have known."

"So please don't get into trouble," he said as he handed me my passport.

Another requirement for gaining entry into the kingdom was that a visitor had to have a sponsor there. In fact, one must have a sponsor before one can obtain a visa. My sponsor was the Saudi government itself.

But, as my friend who arranged the trip explained to me, while scholars and journalists from other countries are first screened by Saudi embassies, which belong to the Foreign Ministry, their actual sponsor inside the kingdom is the Information Ministry.

"Someone from the Information Ministry will meet you at the Riyadh airport and take you to your hotel. The Information Ministry also has your schedule of appointments and will have a car and driver for you."

"Can you tell me the name of the hotel I'll be staying at?" I asked. "I'd like to give the phone number to my wife."

My friend waved his hand with an air of impatience. "I don't know which hotel right off hand. But when you get there, just call her."

That seemed a sensible suggestion.

* * *

Shortly before I left for the kingdom, I noticed that my friend's Israeli professor had published a blistering op-ed piece in *The New York Times* declaring that Saudi Arabia was not a reliable ally for America. I was even more impressed that my friend had chosen to work on his Ph.D. dissertation with someone with whom he obviously must have something of an adversarial relationship.

I left for Riyadh in mid-April 1984. Back then, there were no direct flights from Washington, D.C.--where I lived--to Riyadh. I had to fly to New York's John F. Kennedy airport and get the Saudia Airlines flight that went non-stop to Jeddah and then on to Riyadh.

The flight was long and boring, but Saudia is a decent airline. They show two movies on the eleven hour trip and serve better food than most American airlines. But they don't serve alcohol.

A lot of women, including Arab women, got on board in New York. Many of them were wearing colorful, expensive Western clothes. Except for some of the older ones, none of them had their hair covered. I had always heard that Saudi women wore black garments that covered them from head to toe, leaving only their eyes uncovered at most. Perhaps these were not Saudi women, I thought.

Shortly before we landed in Jeddah, an announcement was made over the loudspeaker: "We have now entered Saudi airspace." There was a rustling of fabric throughout the aircraft. Most of the Arab women were putting on black scarves, face masks, and robes over their Western clothes. It turns out they were Saudis after all.

When we arrived in Jeddah, everyone had to get off the aircraft and go through immigration and customs. For the Riyadh-bound passengers, however, customs only inspected our hand luggage. Our checked bags would be inspected in Riyadh, thus necessitating us to go through the time-consuming customs process twice. But in my case, this second customs inspection did not take very long as my checked baggage did not arrive.

I was not surprised. I have often found that no matter how long the interval between the arrival of my flight at JFK airport and the departure of my next flight, it is almost never long enough for the JFK baggage handlers to get my luggage from one aircraft to the other. So I had learned from previous experience to pack a lot of clothes in my hand luggage.

From the customs area I went to the arrival hall where a crowd of people were waiting for passengers. There must have been a dozen men holding signs with names written on them for people who they were sent to meet but did not know by sight. None of the signs, however, had my name.

I found a comfortable chair to wait in until my contact arrived. In the meantime, I watched as others emerged from the customs area. It appeared somewhat incongruous to see some of the young Saudi women all in black but wearing gray, white, or red high-heeled shoes.

An hour passed.

I hoped that my contact would arrive soon. But there were others who also seemed to be waiting for someone to pick them up. And some of the men with signs bearing the names of arriving passengers were also waiting still. One came over to me and asked whether my name wasn't the name on his sign. I wondered where I would have been taken if I had said, "Yes, that's me! I must not have seen you when I came out."

A second hour passed.

Perhaps visitors sponsored by the Information Ministry were coming in on several flights and we would all be met as a group when the last one arrived. This is what I hoped, but I was beginning to worry that no one would come at all. I had no idea which hotel I was supposed to go to.

A third hour passed.

All the other arriving passengers waiting for rides had either been met or had taken taxis. The men with the signs had either found their parties or had given up and left. No other flights were due in for a couple of hours and the arrival hall was practically deserted.

A friend of mine at the State Department in Washington had given me the number of an American diplomat at what was then the U.S. embassy liaison office in Riyadh whom he said I should look up. The main U.S. embassy--as well as the embassies of all other countries and the Saudi Foreign Ministry--were still located in Jeddah back then. The founder of Saudi Arabia, King `Abd al-Aziz "Ibn Sa`ud" did not want foreign embassies in his capital, Riyadh, and so kept them at a distance. In recent years, though, the Saudi government allowed embassies to maintain liaison offices in Riyadh which steadily grew in size. Soon the embassies as well as the Foreign Ministry itself would all formally move to Riyadh.

Despite the late hour, I decided to call the American diplomat for advice on whether I should continue to wait or try to find a hotel on my own. When I told him my situation, he said he'd send a car and driver to pick me up.

About twenty minutes later, I was picked up in an embassy vehicle and we drove into town looking for a hotel. The first one we stopped at not only had no reservation for me, but no rooms available. The second one had no reservation for me either, but did have one small room open. I took it.

Before going to bed, I called my friend at the Saudi embassy back in Washington to tell him what happened. He expressed annoyance with the Information Ministry and said that he'd make some phone calls for me.

He was as good as his word. The next morning, a short, plump gentleman knocked on my door and announced himself as Mr. Asiri from the Information Ministry. He indicated that I should hurry because the office director in charge of foreign guests wanted to see me as soon as possible. At the hotel entrance, a car and driver were waiting for us. I began to feel like a VIP since I now had a car and two assistants.

The feeling didn't last long. When we got to the Information Ministry, I was taken to a large room. About twenty people from different countries were sitting in chairs and couches along the walls. There was a large desk at the far end of the room where the office director sat. Several assistants hovered about him.

After we were introduced, he said, "Oh yes, I heard you might be coming.

What is it you want to do here in the kingdom?"

This was not very auspicious beginning. I replied that the Saudi embassy in Washington had said that a schedule had been arranged for me.

"There is no schedule for you," the office director informed me. "We never make a schedule for anyone until they actually arrive in the kingdom."

As politely as I could, I enquired as to why that was the case. "Because we don't want to make appointments with busy people for someone who might not actually show up," he responded brusquely.

He then asked me who I wanted to see and what I wanted to talk about. I told him that I was writing a book about Soviet policy toward the region and hoped to talk to officials at the Foreign and Defense Ministries. "Why do you want to write a book about *that*?" he asked irritably. But before I could answer, he said, "Have a seat and I'll see what I can do."

All the other foreigners in the room were in the same position as me: they had been invited to the kingdom by the Saudi embassy located in their country, but found out that nothing had been arranged for them once they arrived in Riyadh. Some had been coming back to this office for several days without having obtained a single appointment with anyone they had asked to see. The Saudi government was even paying the entire cost of the trip, including airfare and hotel, for many of them.

This last group was especially confused. Why had the Saudi government gone to the expense of bringing them here to sit around and wait in this office? One well known Arab-American professor, whose book I had read for a history course when I was an undergraduate, was particularly distraught.

All us foreigners grumbled among ourselves while we watched the office director answer the five phones on his desk. They all had different rings. Sometimes, they all would ring at once, making a particularly cacophonous symphony. Clerks came in and out with papers. After an hour, the office director sent us all back to our hotels, saying there would be news for each of us tomorrow "for sure." This was not a good beginning.

* * *

One of the miseries of traveling alone is often having to eat by oneself in hotel restaurants. Even if the food is good, seeing the same menu over and over becomes tedious. The most boring part, though, is the long period of time between ordering the meal and its arrival when there is literally nothing to do but wait. Usually, I remember to bring something to read in order to fill the time, but today I had forgotten. Under these circumstances, the only thing you can do--whether you want to or not--is to listen in on other peoples' conversations.

When I had come into the dining room, there was another American sitting alone at a table near mine. He was middle aged and was, I would soon learn, a businessman. After awhile, he was joined by a much younger Saudi man. The young Saudi's voice could be heard quite clearly, but the American's was muffled. As soon as the young Saudi sat down, however, it was evident from his facial expressions that the American was unhappy with him.

After a few minutes listening to the American, the Saudi responded in a tired voice, "Doing business here takes more time than in America. If you want to do business here, you have to do things the Saudi way."

"Snivel, snivel, snivel, snivel!" (That's all I could hear.)

"I *am* trying to help you. Do you think I would be here if I wasn't?"

"Snivel, snivel, snivel!"

"Oh, you think I don't want to help you? Well, you're free to work with someone else." The younger man clicked his tongue at the older one as if the latter were a child. "You need to have a better attitude."

"Snivel, snivel!" The American really seemed pathetic.

I was getting the impression that waiting long periods to accomplish anything was the norm for foreign visitors here--maybe for everyone.

* * *

Dick, my contact at the U.S. embassy liaison office, sent a land rover to my hotel that afternoon in order to bring me to his office. When I arrived, he explained that they could be generous with their vehicles because Saudi custom necessitated that they keep a large number on hand. Since women are not allowed to drive in the kingdom, transport for female staff to and from the office had to be provided. But except for the morning and evening "rush hours," the vehicles and their drivers were relatively idle.

Dick also explained that my experience with the Information Ministry was typical. He doubted they would make any substantive appointments for me, especially with anyone at the Foreign Ministry; the two ministries were constantly at odds with each other. He said he would try to help, but the only way I was going to get any appointments with high level officials was to call the Saudi embassy back in Washington and ask my friend there to make them!

* * *

When it was time for me to return to my hotel, Dick again arranged for me to go in an embassy vehicle. Since it had become evening "rush hour," there was another passenger for the land rover whose home was on the way back to my hotel. Her name was Jasmina; she was from Jordan, and she served as an Arabic tutor to the staff members at the liaison office. Like all other Arab women I saw outdoors in Riyadh, she was dressed completely in black.

When the land rover pulled up for us, she got into the back seat. I started to get in beside her when the driver, a young Egyptian, stopped me. "No, no! You must sit in the front seat with me!"

Jasmina laughed. As we were driving along, she explained to me that it was illegal for a man and a woman who were not related to sit together on the same car seat. "It is considered to be `illegal intimacy.'"

Before we dropped her off, she told me that life was much less restrictive for women in Jordan, but it was very difficult to find work there, so she came to Saudi Arabia. Foreign embassies were some of the few places in Saudi Arabia where men and women could work together; Saudi laws which kept the work place segregated could not be applied to embassies.

Our Egyptian driver looked very nervous until we dropped Jasmina off. He later informed me that being caught by the Islamic police even talking with an unrelated woman could lead to very unpleasant consequences. It was hard for me to believe, but I could see that his fear was real.

* * *

Later that evening, I called my friend back at the Saudi embassy in Washington. He groaned when I told him that the Information Ministry had made no appointments for me. "Why do they do this to us?" he asked.

He told me that someone in the Foreign Ministry in Jeddah would set up my appointments without reference to the Information Ministry. He advised me not to mention this to the Information Ministry people for fear that they would insist on their bureaucratic prerogative of being in charge of foreign visitors, and cancel my appointments just to spite the Foreign Ministry.

* * *

That night, I had dinner with Larry, a businessman from Singapore whose company sold computerized microfilming systems. We had met on the flight from Jeddah to Riyadh. I had mentioned to him that after a week in Riyadh, I would be going on to Kuwait. He told me that he had been trying to get a visa to Kuwait for years, but had been unsuccessful. He seemed to think that since I had obtained a Kuwaiti visa for myself, I could somehow help him get one too. Although I kept telling him that I couldn't help him, he insisted on inviting me to dinner one night while I was in Riyadh. At dinner, he described some of the peculiarities of doing business in the kingdom.

"The Saudis become very angry if they find out you are charging them higher prices than you charge customers in other countries," said Larry. I was about to say that I could not blame them when Larry continued, "The problem, however, is that it costs more to do business here than in other countries. In order to make the same profit as we do elsewhere, we must charge the Saudis more."

We were at a Thai restaurant. We were sitting, of course, in the "men only" section of the restaurant. The only other section was "families only" (like all other Saudi restaurants, this one could not accommodate unrelated men and women or even women alone).

We were each drinking our third non-alcoholic beer, wishing that it was the real thing. "The Saudis have a huge bureaucracy to ensure that foreign businessmen do not cheat them. Unfortunately, foreign businessmen have no protection against unscrupulous Saudi practices."

I asked him to tell me about these.

"It can start at the very beginning of the sales process," he said. "A Saudi organization will announce it wishes to purchase a particular product or service and call for bids. But in order to submit a bid, a company must pay a substantial fee--often several thousand dollars--for the bid to be considered. Submission fees from the losing companies are not returned. Sometimes the Saudi organization will accept none of the bids, but will keep all of the fees anyway.

"When a bid actually is accepted, there are more pitfalls. The Saudis require that their suppliers deposit with them ten percent of the total value of the contract up front. The purpose of this deposit is to ensure prompt delivery according to the terms of the contract. But the Saudis do not consider products to be delivered when they arrive in port. The products have to clear customs and be delivered to the purchasing organization."

"That doesn't seem unreasonable," I remarked.

"But if the head of the purchasing organization is corrupt," Larry pointed out, "he may ask for part of the ten percent deposit. If you don't agree, he may have contacts in the customs office who can delay clearance of your shipment. So in order not to lose the entire deposit, you have to give part of it to the head of the purchasing organization. Usually they'll settle for a third to a half, but sometimes they want even more.

"Finally, when you have overcome whatever obstacles they put in your way and you make your delivery or complete your project, there is the little matter of getting paid. They are very slow to pay, and there is no way to make them hurry. After all, if you want to do business with them again, you don't want to antagonize them.

"What the Saudis don't seem to realize, though, is that it is their practices that add to the cost of the goods and services they buy. When calculating what price to charge, every company has to factor in the cost of high bid submission fees, split or lost promptness deposits, and the cost to a company of borrowing money to pay its expenses until the delayed final payments are made. The Saudis think they're being discriminated against, but it is their own fault that they pay more."

"If it is so difficult to do business here, why bother?" I asked.

"You can make money here," he replied, "but you need a lot of patience. Doing business with the Saudis is like dealing with children."

* * *

The next morning, Mr. Asiri showed up unexpectedly at eight o'clock. "Any appointments?" I asked.

"First, we are going for a drive outside of town, then we will go back to the ministry and see about your schedule."

From this as well as other drives through the city, I had begun to form an impression of Riyadh. The capital reminded me very much of Southern California, where I grew up. All the buildings and highways were relatively new. The palaces of the various princes and princesses seemed especially new, and struck me as being similar to the nouveau riche mansions in Beverly Hills (many of which, of course, were built by wealthy Saudis). The sky was often brown, just as was the sky in Southern California when I lived there. People here said the brown sky was dust, but it looked like smog to me. Certainly, there were enough large American cars here to produce it. Indeed, Saudi Arabia was the only country I have visited in this part of the world where American cars seemed most prevalent, unlike Japanese ones everywhere else.

Also like Southern California, it struck me that very little thought seems to have been given to preserving old buildings in Saudi Arabia. When I mentioned this at the embassy liaison office, someone there remarked, "They have no old buildings to preserve in Riyadh since before these new ones were put up, the Saudis all lived in tents."

But outside of the capital, there were some old buildings being restored. Mr. Asiri took me to Daraiyah, a previous Saudi capital, which was about twenty miles from Riyadh. Daraiyah had been the capital when the Saudi family first came to rule much of what is now the desert kingdom in the late eighteenth century. The city, however, was destroyed in 1819 by the forces of Muhammad Ali, the ambitious Ottoman viceroy of Egypt whom the sultan in Istanbul had sent to drive the Saudis out of the holy cities of Mecca and Medina.

When we got there, an Egyptian archaeologist showed me around the site. The old city was constructed primarily from what looked to me like adobe, only it was grayish. Some of the buildings had been three stories tall. There seemed to be a pattern in the construction: the ground floor of the buildings had doorways but no windows. The next floor usually did not have windows either, but had small triangular openings at regular intervals--apparently for circulation. Only on the third floor were there usually windows as well as more triangular openings.

It was clear that Daraiyah had never been a grand city on the Egyptian scale--the scarcity of water, and consequently of agricultural produce--would not permit it to grow very large. Still, it was an evocative place. Unlike Southern Californiaesque Riyadh, Daraiyah seemed like something from *Arabian Nights*. I took lots of photographs.

The archaeologist told me that the old capital was being restored very slowly. Part of the problem was that there was only one surviving text from the late eighteenth century with a detailed description of Daraiyah and life there at that time. It just so happened, however, that the text's anonymous author was highly critical of the Saudi family and the rigid form of Islam which it upheld. Thus, while the Saudi ruling family now wanted to restore the splendors of the dynasty's founders, it could not bring itself to completely trust a restoration project based on an anti-Saudi manuscript. So the project proceeded in fits and starts.

* * *

Mr. Asiri and I went back to the Information Ministry. I took a seat. Most of the same crowd from yesterday was there again. There were a few new arrivals as well. No one seemed to be making any progress.

The office director told me twice that he should have word about my schedule in a few minutes . . . in a few minutes. After an hour and a half, a clerk came bustling into the room and said something I could not catch in Arabic to the office director. He turned to me and said, "There is a telephone call for you in the room across the hall. He," meaning the clerk, "will show you the way."

Movement at last! The other foreign visitors sat up at this. I followed the clerk. But by the time I reached the phone, the line was dead. Crestfallen, I went back to the office director to report what had happened. "Do you know who it was who was trying to call me?" I asked. "Maybe I can try to call him back."

"I cannot say," he answered ambiguously. Apparently having decided that this had been enough excitement for me today, he told Mr. Asiri to take me back to my hotel.

* * *

After another lonely lunch, I checked the front desk to see if I had any messages. There was nothing from the Foreign Ministry, but there was one from Dick. When I called, he told me that the Marine guards were throwing a party that evening and I was invited. He also invited me to a lunch at his home two days hence with some local notables. I gratefully accepted both invitations.

That evening, a land rover came by to collect me. Dick and another American diplomat were already inside. We drove to the site of the party. After parking on a residential street, we went through a metal gate in a high wall. On the other side was a crowd of Westerners, mostly wearing swim suits. Everyone seemed to be drinking beer, wine, or something harder. We immediately went into the house where the Marines had their bar and obtained beers for ourselves. "This isn't a problem?" I asked.

"The Saudi government doesn't stop embassies from importing alcohol," Dick explained. We went back outside. I watched as a group of American women came through the metal gate. They came in wearing scarves and what looked like long, baggy robes. Within seconds, they whipped these off and were dressed only in bikinis.

The main topic of conversation among the people I met was alcohol. Many of the Westerners present were not diplomats, and so obtaining alcohol was more difficult and more dangerous for them: they did not enjoy diplomatic immunity. People talked about their suppliers, the cost, the merits and demerits of homebrew, and what had happened to people caught buying or selling it. I had never thought of alcohol as a drug, but the way people talked about it here reminded me of how students talked about marijuana when I was in college.

* * *

The next morning, Mr. Asiri came by much later than he had the previous day. He then took me on something of a tour of the city. He really seemed to want me to have an enjoyable visit.

We went to a modern shopping mall. In the window of one clothing store hung colorful lingerie. Two women in black stood outside the shop staring at it.

We drove to a few other places as well. Remembering my wife's instructions to bring her back some jewelry, I asked if there was a *soukh* where I could buy a gold bracelet.

Mr. Asiri took me to a *soukh*. There were numerous stalls selling different items; goldsmiths were by far the most prevalent type of merchant. This, however, was not a real traditional *soukh* like I had seen in Oman or Yemen with a maze of alleys and people actively bargaining over the price. This Riyadh *soukh* was cleaner, brighter, and more subdued. It reminded me of American townhouse communities that tried to recreate the architecture and ambiance of a country town: somehow it was not the real thing.

At one stall, I found a bracelet that I thought my wife would like. I asked Mr. Asiri to interpret for the goldsmith and me. Unlike previous *soukhs* I had been to, the merchant here did not seem particularly interested in bargaining. I was just telling Mr. Asiri that I would pay the price asked when I noticed beyond him an elderly man wearing black approaching us with a thin stick in his hand. The man stopped a few feet away from Mr. Asiri and stared directly at us.

"Who is that?" I asked.

Turning away from me, Mr. Asiri looked to his right. He gasped when he saw the man and quickly moved from my right to my left so that he was no longer in between me and the man in black. "It is an Islamic policeman. The call to prayer is about to begin. You must complete this transaction immediately." He then walked away from me hurriedly.

I quickly counted out the money and threw it at the merchant. He, in turn, thrust the bracelet at me. I looked over at the man in black again; he was just beginning to raise his stick. I hurried away as fast as I could without actually running until I caught up with Mr. Asiri. He was inside our car with the doors locked.

* * *

We next went to the palace of Prince Salman, the governor of Riyadh, to attend his *majlis*. On virtually every working day, all the leading officials--whether they be mayors, governors, or the king himself--hold a *majlis*. Any

Saudi citizen can attend and petition the prince. I had told Mr. Asiri that I wanted to see a *majlis,* and on his own initiative he took me to this one.

I waited in an anteroom for a while at first since, unlike Saudis, foreigners had to get permission to attend. After permission was granted, I was taken to a large reception hall. There were several dozen Saudi men there already. One large chair stood empty at one end of the room.

The men were milling around talking when suddenly the prince entered with a half dozen of his retainers. The prince sat down in the chair. Three retainers stood to his right while the other three stood to his left.

When the prince entered, the men who had been waiting immediately moved toward the sides of the room. Two more of the prince's retainers moved along the sides of the room quickly passing out the small, handle-less coffee cups which the Saudis favor. Yet two more retainers followed them pouring coffee into them from traditional Arab coffee pots.

The prince was handed a large sheaf of letters. He read the first one and then quietly stated the name of the person who had written it. His retainers then bellowed out the man's name several times.

The man who had been called for approached the prince. The prince said a few words to him which the rest of us could not hear. The man was then led to an exit by one of the retainers. While he was leaving, the prince handed the man's letter to another retainer. Everyone else in the room remained silent during this process.

This process was repeated many times. Usually the petitioner exchanged a few words with the prince and was led away. Sometimes the petitioner was intercepted by a retainer and led out; I concluded that these were the ones whose petitions were denied. In no case did the petitioner attempt to argue with the prince. On two occasions, though, petitioners were led to a back office, apparently to await further discussion. The men with the coffee pots went around twice more to give refills.

After half an hour, the prince abruptly stood up. He handed the large number of letters which he had not yet read to a retainer. The prince and the six retainers left for the back office while others ushered everyone remaining in the reception hall toward the exit. The *majlis* was over. Those whose petitions had not been read would have to come back tomorrow and hope for better luck.

* * *

We then went, as usual, back to the Information Ministry. Again, there was no news. Some of what we now referred to among ourselves as "the gang" were off on tours of the new industrial cities of Yanbu and Jubail. Others were visiting schools. A few had actually gotten appointments at government ministries.

Again, a call came through for me in the other room. The caller was still on the line when I got there this time. I said hello and introduced myself.

"I think I can see you the day after tomorrow," replied a deep voice on the other end.

"Wonderful!" I responded cheerily. "Who is this please?"

The line went dead.

I walked back into the other room. "Is it all arranged?" asked the office director.

"Yes," I answered. I didn't know what else to say. The office director had Mr. Asiri take me back to my hotel.

* * *

That afternoon, I had a call from Dick. He confirmed that the lunch he had arranged for me was still on. He had also made an appointment for me beforehand with an assistant to the director-general of the Gulf Cooperation Council--the regional organization formed by the six Arab Gulf monarchies (Saudi Arabia, Kuwait, Bahrain, Qatar, the United Arab Emirates, and Oman). He would send an embassy vehicle to my hotel tomorrow.

Late that evening, I received another call. A deep male voice said, "The foreign minister, Prince Sa`ud al-Faysal, will receive you tomorrow at ten a.m. in his office."

My friend at the Saudi embassy back in Washington had done it! I thanked my caller but before I could ask where Prince Sa`ud's office was, he hung up.

I called Dick; he was ecstatic. "We have a hard time getting in to see the foreign minister, so your friend really must have pull." He said he'd send an embassy vehicle over earlier tomorrow so that it could take me to all three of my appointments.

The next morning, Mr. Asiri showed up at my room around nine o'clock looking rather forlorn. "This morning we will visit a museum before we go to the ministry."

I told him that I had made my own arrangements for today. And since the U.S. embassy was putting one of their vehicles at my disposal, he was free to attend to more important matters than showing me around.

Mr. Asiri looked suspicious. "What appointments do you have?"

As soon as I told him I was going to see the foreign minister, he telephoned his office. There was a lot of spirited discussion. I remembered too late the advice of my Saudi friend in Washington not to let the Information Ministry know about anything he arranged for me. Maybe they would cancel the appointment.

When he got off the phone, Mr. Asiri asked me, "How did you arrange this?" But before I could answer, he said, "You must go to the appointment with Prince Sa`ud in the Information Ministry's car, not the embassy's."

I explained that this wasn't necessary because I needed the embassy vehicle to take me on to other appointments later.

"And what appointments are they?" I told him, and then he called his office again. After another spirited conversation, he put down the receiver and announced, "You may go to the other appointments in the embassy's car, but you *must* go to Prince Sa`ud's in ours."

I decided there was no point in arguing. At least they hadn't canceled the appointment. We went to the hotel entrance where both vehicles were waiting for me. I explained the situation to the embassy driver. He decided to follow me since he would be taking me to GCC headquarters and to lunch afterward. And so I set off to see the foreign minister in my little motorcade.

When we arrived at the prince's office, Mr. Asiri came in with me and made it clear to the head clerk that the Information Ministry had brought me. We waited in the anteroom together silently until I was called in to see the prince.

* * *

Prince Sa`ud greeted me as I entered. He was a very tall man who spoke English perfectly. He, his assistant, and I were the only ones in the room.

Just recently, the new Saudi ambassador in Washington, Prince Bandar, had had dinner with the Soviet ambassador, Anatoliy Dobrynin. There was much speculation that this presaged the imminent resumption of Saudi-Soviet diplomatic relations (there had been ties between them in the 1920s and 1930s, but not since then). I asked Prince Sa`ud if this was about to occur.

He shook his head and said, "We will only recognize Moscow if it meets certain conditions:

"First," he began, "they must completely withdraw their armed forces from Afghanistan." The Soviets had invaded that country in 1979 to prop up a Marxist regime there against its Muslim opponents.

"Second, they must end all hostile propaganda against Saudi Arabia.

"Third, they must withdraw from Ethiopia and South Yemen." Ethiopia was just across the Red Sea while South Yemen directly bordered on Saudi Arabia. Both had Marxist regimes and a large Soviet military presence.

"Fourth, there must be freedom for Muslims to practice their religion in the USSR.

"But even if they meet all our conditions," the prince added, "relations will not be restored automatically. There must also be the right psychological conditions."

* * *

When the prince said this in 1984, it seemed as if he was setting conditions which he knew the Soviets would never meet (except, possibly, ending hostile propaganda). Saudi-Soviet relations, then, would never be re-established.

In September 1990, though, Prince Sa'ud went to Moscow and met with Eduard Shevardnadze (then the Soviet foreign minister). Saudi-Soviet relations were formally re-established.

By the time this happened, all the conditions which the prince told me that Moscow must meet either had been met or were just about to be. Moscow had long since ended its hostile propaganda against the kingdom. Soviet forces completed their withdrawal from Afghanistan in February 1989. Moscow made no move to halt the self-liquidation of the Marxist regime in South Yemen and its merger under the leadership of non-Marxist North Yemen in May 1990. Moscow had considerably reduced its assistance to Marxist Ethiopia and would end it completely by January 1991 (the regime would be driven out of power a few months later).

In addition, by the time Prince Sa'ud went to Moscow, Muslims were free to practice their religion in the USSR. Much to Saudi dismay, Muslims in the USSR had become so free that a little later many of them would vigorously protest Soviet support for the American-led, UN-sponsored coalition formed to protect the kingdom and expel Iraqi forces from Kuwait.

And last but not least, the Iraqi invasion of Kuwait apparently created the right "psychological conditions:" Riyadh was finally willing to restore diplomatic ties with the USSR in order to make sure Moscow voted its way on UN Security Council resolutions aimed at Iraq--which Moscow did.

Although it seemed impossible in 1984, the Soviets had fulfilled all the Saudi conditions for resuming relations by 1990.

After he listed these conditions back in 1984, I asked the prince whether he thought the Soviets would ever fulfill them.

He smiled and said, "It is in the hands of God."

Saudi Sojourn

* * *

At the end of my interview, I found that Mr. Asiri was sleeping in the anteroom. He accompanied me outside, but then left in his vehicle while I went on in the embassy's. His obligation to show the Information Ministry flag at the Foreign Ministry had successfully been fulfilled.

The meeting at GCC headquarters was nothing special. But lunch that Wednesday afternoon at Dick's was a fun occasion. Dick's house servant (these Foreign Service officers get great perks) plied us all with wine. I was becoming more sympathetic with the Western community's obsession with alcohol. The fact that it was illegal, I realized, definitely enhanced the pleasure of drinking.

Hours later when the party broke up, we were all pretty buzzed. But in one sense it did not matter: there was a car and driver waiting for each of us, so there was no question of attempting to drive under the influence. All I had to do, Dick told me, was maintain a sober decorum going from his front door to the vehicle and from the vehicle to my hotel room, just in case the Islamic police were prowling around.

* * *

Later that day, I learned that my Saudi friend back in Washington had been busy again. The relatively young man who had been appointed head of the newly formed Saudi National Security Office called to invite me to lunch the next day. He said that he would come by my hotel around noon to pick me up.

I was impressed that he had called me himself and that he was willing to spend part of his weekend with me (Thursday and Friday are the weekend in the Muslim world).

I was just getting up at nine the next morning when there was a knock at my door. It was Mr. Asiri. "What are you doing here on the weekend?" I asked.

"Come, we have to go."
"Where?" I asked.
"To a dairy farm."
This was not my idea of fun.
"How far away is it?" I asked.
"An hour," he replied.

I told him about my luncheon appointment at noon, expressed concern that I might be late for it if I visited the dairy, and suggested that Mr. Asiri himself might have better things to do with his weekend than taking me to see some cows.

"But *you* were the one who made this appointment," he replied. "We can't cancel it now."

At first I was confused. Then I remembered: the voice on the telephone a couple of days ago at the Information Ministry must have been the director of the farm. Not wishing to cause any protocol problems or embarrass Mr. Asiri with his boss, I decided I had better go.

Once out of town, we drove through miles and miles of barren desert. Finally, we came to the gate of the dairy farm. Past this, the ground was covered with lush green grass. There were several huge mobile water booms.

We drove up to the farm's office building and went inside to see the director. I was hoping that we could make this a short visit and get back to Riyadh quickly.

But the director had other ideas. He launched into a long harangue in Arabic. Mr. Asiri nodded assent periodically. This lasted fifteen minutes.

Finally, the director addressed me in English. "I was just saying," he told me in an injured tone, "how everyone in the West insisted that Saudi Arabia could not have a dairy farm because ours is a desert country. But here we have one of the largest dairy farms in all the world. The same is true with wheat: people said we could not grow it here, but now we grow so much that we have to export it." He gave me all the statistics. Mr. Asiri continued to nod, though I was beginning to suspect that this was less a sign of assent than of boredom.

The harangue finally came to an end. I glanced furtively at my watch; it was already past 10:30. I was hoping we could head back to town now, but the director insisted that I tour his farm. Before we could say anything, he had called in one of his assistants: a young man from Northern Ireland. The Irishman and I were heading for the door, but Mr. Asiri remained seated.

"Aren't you coming?" I asked.

"I've seen it several times already," he replied.

The Irishman, who seemed just as proud of the farm as the director, showed me the ultra-modern milking chambers. The whole process seemed very well organized. "This is very impressive," I admitted. "How big a profit does the farm make?"

"It makes no profit at all," he responded. "In fact, it operates at an enormous deficit."

"Then what's the point of running it?" I asked. "Wouldn't it be cheaper just to import dairy products from abroad?"

"It would be much cheaper," he answered. "But they want to produce their own milk. They're not worried about making a profit on this."

I explained that I really had to get back to Riyadh, so he took me back to the director's office. But before letting me leave, the director insisted that I drink a small carton of his farm's most prized product--*laban* (a sort of buttermilk which is very popular among Saudis). I thanked him and said that I'd drink it in the car (I planned to give it to either Mr. Asiri or the driver). But the director insisted I drink it here. Fearing I would not be allowed to leave until I drank it, I opened the carton and took a sip. It was incredibly sour. No one else in the room was drinking it, but they all insisted that I had to finish it. I did, trying unsuccessfully to prevent my face from puckering.

They all laughed heartily. "I think for Westerners, *laban* is an acquired taste," said the director.

Mr. Asiri and I said good-bye and left. The sour *laban* taste remained in my mouth all during the trip back. Just as we stopped at my hotel, Mr. Asiri offered me two more cartons of *laban*. I insisted that he take them to his family.

I was now fifteen minutes late for my luncheon appointment. I hoped that the person I was to meet would be late too, but I soon learned that he had arrived on time. Furthermore, he had brought a prince with him. "According to the common stereotype," said one of them when we met, "Americans are always on time and Saudis are always late. But this time it is the opposite."

I had the feeling that neither of them had ever been kept waiting before--at least, not by somebody outside the royal family. I apologized profusely.

* * *

At lunch, the prince--like every other Arab I have ever met--wanted to talk about American support for Israel. But unlike so many Arabs with whom I discussed this with, the prince was not strident or angry. Instead, he appeared sad and puzzled.

"Whenever I travel to America or Western Europe," he said, "one of the things that constantly surprises me is the old elite there. They never hesitate to disparage Jews or to let me know how they find Jews distasteful. Maybe they say this because that's what they think Arabs want to hear.

"But we Arabs don't feel that way about Jews," he continued. "In fact, we genuinely sympathize with them over the cruel treatment they have received, especially at the hands of the Nazis. What we can't understand is how the Jewish nation, which has experienced so much suffering, can callously turn around and inflict so much suffering on the Palestinians.

"And even if Jews cannot see the contradiction, why don't Americans? Yours is a country supposedly dedicated to promoting freedom and democracy. And yet you not only tolerate Israeli occupation of Arab territories where the population clearly doesn't want to be ruled by Israel, but you actually provide Israel with the military and economic assistance which allows it to maintain this rule.

"Why do you do it? What American interests are served?"

I told him how American conservatives saw Israel as America's most reliable ally in a region where the Soviet Union had made considerable inroads.

He just laughed. "But if the Soviets have succeeded at making inroads here, it is because you Americans support Israel. If you didn't support Israel, there would have been almost no popular sympathy for the USSR. As it is, American support for Israel only makes it difficult for conservative Arab governments to cooperate with the U.S. The fact that we cooperate with Israel's primary supporter helps our opponents challenge our legitimacy. Is that in your interests?"

I explained that for the American public, it wasn't simply a question of interests. There was tremendous sympathy in America for the Jews because of the atrocities they had experienced during World War II.

"Well, then why didn't you simply allow the Jews of Europe to emigrate to the United States?"

I responded that many European Jews--especially those in the Zionist movement--felt that being a minority in another nation would not allow them sufficient protection if the majority turned against them. They felt that they needed to have their own state.

"I sympathize with that argument," said the prince. "But if Germany was the state primarily responsible for persecuting the Jews, why weren't they given part of German territory? Why should the Arabs have to compensate the Jews for what they suffered at the hands of the Germans and other Europeans?"

I reminded him how the Zionist movement had evolved. First, it was willing to accept a homeland practically anywhere; Uganda in East Africa was being seriously considered at the turn of the century. But when the Ottoman Empire, which included Palestine, allied with Germany during World War I, the Zionists saw they had the opportunity to create a Jewish homeland in what was historical Israel at the end of the war.

"But this type of claim is preposterous," said the prince. "If the Jews can displace the population of Palestine and set up their own state because a

Jewish state existed there over two thousand years ago, does this mean other nations can do the same? Should the native Americans be allowed to expel the rest of the American population? If you allow this type of claim, you are opening up Pandora's box--especially since several nations may have occupied a given territory over the course of history. How do you decide which claim is valid?

"Look," he said, "we Arabs are no longer demanding that Israel cease to exist, even though we think its creation was illegitimate. There is now a country with an overwhelming Jewish majority within the 1967 borders. But Jews do not constitute the majority in the West Bank and Gaza Strip. The Palestinian majority there does not want to be ruled by Israel. Is the security of Israel so all-important that you Americans are willing to allow the Israelis to rule over the Palestinians against their will indefinitely? Do you think that the situation is somehow going to get better if this state of affairs is allowed to continue?"

As the Israeli-Palestinian peace process that got under way a decade later showed, even the Israelis would come to accept the prince's logic.

* * *

I stayed inside the hotel all day Friday. I didn't want to bother any of my new acquaintances, especially since none of them had extended me any invitations for that day. Nor did I venture out on my own. Outside of private homes, there is not a lot of entertainment to be found in Riyadh. There are no movie theaters, no discos, no bars. There are book stores, but their inventories tend to be extremely limited as well as uninteresting. Nor did just walking around on my own seem like a good idea; I found myself worrying that the all-pervasive Islamic police might somehow take offense at the very sight of me.

So I stayed in my room and watched the hotel's in-house video, read a novel, and worked on writing up my notes. At one point, though, I went up to the highest floor in the hotel and took photographs of the city from the windows there. I came down to the lobby with my camera slung around my neck. The Pakistani desk clerk ordered me to take it back to my room at once. He said that if the Islamic police saw me, smashing the camera was the minimum they would do. I might also have to exchange my hotel room for a prison cell.

I didn't know whether he was exaggerating. But I didn't want to put his warning to the test either. So the camera went back to my room and inside my suitcase.

***

The next three days--my last in the kingdom on this trip--were extremely busy. Both the Saudi embassy in Washington and the U.S. embassy liaison office in Riyadh had been able to arrange several more appointments for me--including ones with two more ministers and even the chief of intelligence, Prince Turki al-Faysal (the brother of the foreign minister). In addition, I received several calls from people wanting an appointment with me. In countries like Saudi Arabia where the media carries very little substantive news, those who do meet with policy-makers become "living newspapers" of a sort. In other words, people called not because they were particularly interested in me, but because they wanted to learn from me what the foreign minister had had to say.

But before I saw any of them, Mr. Asiri brought me to see the office director at the Information Ministry early Saturday morning. It was so early that no other foreign visitors were there yet. Before I could ask him about it, he asked me, "What is your schedule?" He then let me know that "it is better" to go in the Information Ministry's vehicle to see anyone important.

***

Later that day, I went to King Sa'ud University where the U.S. Information Service branch of the embassy had arranged for me to give a seminar on Soviet policy toward the region. No students attended the seminar; only professors. During the discussion after my presentation, I happened to mention that I had recently visited Oman, Saudi Arabia's southeastern neighbor. I was quite surprised to hear all the Saudi professors then express utter contempt for Oman.

"The Omani sultan is completely incompetent," said one.

"The entire ruling family there is a pack of fools," said another.

"If they weren't members of a ruling family, none of them could even get jobs as garbage collectors," said a third.

They continued in this vein:

"There is no academic freedom at their university."

"It is named after the sultan, of course--just like everything else in that miserable country."

"Foreigners run everything there. The sultan does not want to give important jobs to too many Omanis for fear they'll band together and overthrow him."

"Oman cannot be said to be an independent country at all. It is really a

Western colony."

"The sultan poses as a pious Islamic leader. But it is just a pose."

They went on and on. None of the Saudi professors had anything good to say about Oman.

After the seminar, one of the younger Saudi professors walked me out to where my car and driver were waiting. As we approached the car, I asked him, "Why are you all so negative about Oman?"

"Oman? We weren't talking about Oman," he responded.

"Then what were you talking about?"

He immediately turned around and walked back toward his office.

* * *

On the day I left Saudi Arabia, I visited the minister whose son back at the Saudi embassy in Washington had arranged this visit for me. When I entered his office, there was only one piece of paper on the minister's desk: a copy of the anti-Saudi op-ed piece by his son's Israeli professor. Upon seeing this, I immediately told the minister how much I respected his son for having the author of this article on his dissertation committee. Many Saudi graduate students had the reputation for picking universities and professors who would not demand very much of them. His son was quite obviously an exception.

The minister's smile changed to a look of disbelief. "Do you mean to tell me that *this* man is my son's professor?" he asked, pointing at the article. I suddenly realized that I had let the cat out of the bag.

"How could my son do this?" he cried. "This man has no respect whatsoever for our country!

"If you are really my son's friend," he continued, "you will tell him that he will not have much of a career in the kingdom if he has this man on his committee!"

"But he also has an Arab scholar as the chair of his committee," I pointed out.

"That doesn't matter!" the father insisted. "You tell him what I said!"

I felt miserable. My friend had worked hard to get me into the kingdom as well as arrange my meetings with various high level officials. And in return I got him in trouble with his father. But I had no way of knowing that he hadn't told his father about which professors he was working with.

* * *

Before escorting me to the airport that afternoon, Mr. Asiri took me to the Information Ministry one last time to say good-bye to the office director. I told him that my visit to Saudi Arabia had been extremely productive, and I thanked him for the role he had played in it.

Instead of interpreting my remarks as being sarcastic (as they were intended), he stated in the friendliest tone I had heard him speak in how delighted he had been to assist me. He even invited me to "come back again" so he could "arrange an even better schedule." I believe he had convinced himself that he in fact had arranged all my appointments for me.

Before I left, though, he said he wanted to give me a small present. He made a brief phone call, and then a clerk came into the room carrying six cartons of *laban*. I started to thank him, trying not to let my consternation show, but everyone in the office burst out laughing. Mr. Asiri had apparently told them all about what happened at the dairy farm.

And on that sour note, Mr. Asiri took me to the airport.

* * *

Shortly after returning to Washington, I called my friend at the Saudi embassy to thank him for all his hard work. He was in a happy mood, but I soon changed that. "Have you spoken to your father recently?" I asked.

"No," he responded warily. "Why?"

"I think you had better talk to him."

"Is something wrong?" he asked.

"I think you should give him a call."

"I'll call him immediately," said my friend.

An hour later, my friend called me back. The first thing he said was, "Why did you tell him?" He was not happy.

"I'm sorry," I replied, "but I thought he already knew."

"Well, he does now. I've only just finished talking with him. He yelled at me the entire time."

"So what was the outcome?" I asked.

"We reached our usual compromise: I gave in completely."

My friend never did finish his dissertation. But he did go on to become an important official in the Saudi government. He has not, however, offered to arrange another visit to the kingdom for me.

Kuwaiti and Non-Kuwaiti

When I found out that I would be going to Saudi Arabia, I decided to try to go to Kuwait as well. But everyone told me that getting a Kuwaiti visa was very difficult--even more difficult than getting a Saudi one. I didn't know any Kuwaitis. So I got hold of the *Diplomatic List*--the State Department publication which identifies all the accredited diplomats in Washington. I turned to the page where Kuwait was listed and decided to call the number three man. After I explained who I was and what I wanted to his secretary, he took my call. We had a friendly chat, at the end of which he asked me to come visit him at his office the following week, which I did. I apparently passed muster, for at the end of the meeting he told me to put my request in writing and said that he would attach his recommendation that I be admitted before forwarding it on to Kuwait City.

A few weeks later, I received a letter stating that my proposed visit to Kuwait had been approved. A week before embarking on this trip (first to Saudi Arabia and then to Kuwait), I went back to the Kuwaiti embassy to get my visa. I filled out a form and handed it and my passport to my contact there. A few minutes later, my passport was handed back to me with a newly stamped Kuwaiti visa. I was truly impressed with how quickly and efficiently the Kuwaitis had handled everything--even though they really did not know me.

But just as I was preparing to leave, my new Kuwaiti friend said, "You have approval to go to Kuwait. But we still have not received final word from the Information Ministry whether they can host you on the days you plan to be there. But I think it will be all right. Don't worry about it."

So I didn't. But since I had not heard any news after this, I telephoned the Kuwaiti embassy the same day in April 1984 that I was flying to Saudi Arabia. My friend seemed a little embarrassed. "We haven't actually heard yet from the Information Ministry. But I'm sure everything will be fine. Give me a call from Riyadh next week to make sure."

Just as with my visit to Kuwait, my visit to Saudi Arabia was initiated by the embassy in Washington but once in the country I was the guest of the Information Ministry. And, as I have described elsewhere, this arrangement was not very successful in Saudi Arabia. The Saudi Information Ministry did not meet me at the airport, arrange for a hotel, or set up any appointments as I was told it would. I had to arrange everything myself mainly by telephoning the Saudi embassy back in Washington. This took a lot of time and money. I was afraid that the same situation might confront me again in Kuwait--only it would be worse since I had less time there than in Saudi Arabia.

While I was still in Riyadh, then, I called the Kuwaiti embassy back in Washington. My friend's tone of voice informed me that things were not right. "We did finally hear from the Information Ministry. It turns out that your visit comes at an inconvenient time for them. They have asked that you come to Kuwait in about two months from now."

I told him that I did not have the money for another trip to the Middle East. Such a consideration seemed to come as a complete surprise to him. "I tell you what," he said. "Why don't you call the Information Ministry in Kuwait yourself. Maybe if you explain the situation to them, they will change their mind."

He gave me the name and number of the man in charge of visitors like me. When I finally got through to him and identified myself, he immediately put me on hold. After awhile, a woman's voice came on the line. I explained to her that this was the best time for me to come to Kuwait since I didn't have the money to fly home and then come back to Kuwait later.

"Oh, you're in Saudi Arabia already," she commented. "We thought you were coming to Kuwait first." I detected a note of hurt national pride in her voice. I decided to try and use this to my advantage. I told her what a wonderful time I was having in Saudi Arabia, how I had been received by the foreign minister and several other Saudi bigwigs. I didn't mention the extreme difficulty I had experienced in making these appointments.

"It would be a pity if you could not come to Kuwait," she said slowly. "You may as well come now. I'm not sure what we can arrange for you on such short notice, but we will try to arrange something." My strategy worked!

* * *

When I arrived in Kuwait on the flight from Riyadh, everything went like clockwork. As I passed through immigration, an announcement over the public address system stated that someone was waiting for me in the terminal. The couple who met me drove me straight to my hotel. A big basket of fruit was in my room. The next morning at eight o'clock, I was woken by a call from the Information Ministry saying that a car and driver would pick me up in an hour. The car and driver appeared precisely on time (rare in this part of the world) and I was taken to the office of the woman whom I had spoken to on the phone when I was in Saudi Arabia.

After we shook hands (something that is either not allowed or simply does not happen between unrelated men and women in many countries neighboring Kuwait), she told me that she had arranged for me to visit Kuwait University today and to meet tomorrow first with the under secretary of state for foreign affairs and then the minister of state for cabinet affairs. She apologized for not having arranged any other appointments yet, and then asked me if there was anything else I would like her to try to set up.

I was astounded. Neither before nor since has an information ministry in the Middle East ever been so helpful. This was also the only country where the person in charge of setting up my appointments was a woman.

* * *

Kuwait is different from the other Gulf monarchies with respect to its treatment of women. In Saudi Arabia, women and men are not allowed to work together. Elsewhere in the region, women can work, but they are usually not found in important positions. Their demeanor in the work place is usually reticent, at least toward men. In Kuwait, though, women are found in important positions and they are not shy about asserting themselves. One contrast between Saudi Arabia and Kuwait illustrates the starkly different status that women have in each country. In Saudi Arabia, women are not allowed to leave the house without being veiled or to drive cars at all. In Kuwait, women are not required to veil and are allowed to drive. There is one restriction, though, with regard to driving: they must not impair their ability to see by covering their eyes.

Yet while Kuwait was far more relaxed than Saudi Arabia with regard to freedom for women, it was far more tense in another. In Saudi Arabia, there seemed to be little concern about Iraqi or Iranian subversion despite the fact that the fierce Iran-Iraq war was taking place so close to it. There were no security checks at the entrance of government or any other buildings in Riyadh when I visited. Airport security did not seem particularly tight either.

In Kuwait, by contrast, there were security posts everywhere. Visitors had to run a gauntlet of metal detectors and guards who frisked them up and down not only to enter government buildings, but virtually all other large buildings too. Of course, it was not surprising that the Kuwaiti government was concerned about security, since the war was taking place right smack on this tiny country's northern border. The Iranians had dropped a few bombs on Kuwait already. Although Iraq was then on the defensive against Iran, it too was seen as a threat. But what had really created a tense atmosphere was the bombing of the American and French embassies by terrorists in December 1983, just a few months before my visit.

Security around what was left of the U.S. embassy was especially tight. There were several guards and an armored vehicle with a machine gun mounted on it outside the main gate. After my driver and I parked and were walking toward the entrance, the guards pointed their rifles at us and shouted. They insisted that we move our car from the embassy side of the street to the other side. This was the first and only time I have ever had a rifle pointed at me outside Iraq (there it happened repeatedly each and every time I went outside).

* * *

When I did not have appointments, I spent a lot of time watching the television in my room. The dramas that America exports are primarily detective shows--and the image of America they portray is of an extraordinarily violent nation where people are prone to shoot on the slightest provocation and where individuals must take the law into their own hands because the police cannot or will not do much of anything about crime. I, for one, have never once met a private detective. Maybe my circle of acquaintance is limited, but no one I know has met one either. And yet foreigners watching American television programs could understandably get the impression that this is the most common profession in the U.S. since they are featured in most of our dramas.

Kuwaiti television programming, which is all controlled by the state, definitely does not give the impression that there is any violence in Kuwait. In fact, Kuwaiti (or other Arab Gulf) television programming conveys the image of a happy, peaceful, prosperous society in which nothing at all ever goes wrong. There were two aspects of Kuwaiti television, however, which I found particularly distinctive.

One was the news programming. Virtually the entire newscasts which I saw were devoted to coverage of visiting foreign delegations to Kuwait. The stories were virtually all the same. The newscaster would identify the foreign visitors--such as the Hungarian minister of foreign economic relations, or someone equally obscure, and his entourage. The camera would show the visitors getting into limousines at their hotel in Kuwait. It would then focus on the head of the delegation riding in the limo. Then the visitors would be shown getting out of their limos at the amir's palace. The most coverage would be devoted to the delegation sitting with the amir in his divan, or meeting room. Sometimes the crown prince would attend. Sometimes the delegation would meet with him separately. But on none of these occasions was any conversation between the foreign delegation and the Kuwaiti leadership broadcast; music would be played while the camera showed them smiling and nodding.

A typical newscast might cover two or three such delegations, each meeting with the amir in the same room where they appear to be chatting politely. At first, I couldn't figure out what was the point of broadcasting these scenes repeatedly if nothing was said about the substance of the talks. But, of course, Arab governments tend not to reveal much about the substance of their talks with other governments. The purpose of this coverage, I concluded, was to show the Kuwaiti audience how foreign countries treated the Kuwaiti government with great deference and respect.

Seeing this scene repeatedly, however, struck me as demonstrative less of the Kuwaiti leadership's importance than of its vanity. Still, the Kuwaiti leadership did come across looking relatively benign compared to the gun-toting Saddam Hussein whose image was ever-present on the Iraqi television broadcasts which could easily be seen in Kuwait.

The other aspect of Kuwaiti television which I found interesting was the entertainment programming. Several of the locally produced shows I saw focused on "old Kuwait"--that is, pre-oil Kuwait. There was one musical in particular which struck me: it portrayed the difficult life of Kuwaiti pearl divers--one of the main sources of income before the oil boom. Indeed, old Kuwait is a theme that is featured not only on television, but in many other forms. Book stores and magazine stands sell several different picture books featuring old black and white photos. Many buildings I visited had exhibitions of similar photos. Kuwaitis often have old pictures of their relatives in their offices. The Kuwaiti government has also gone to considerable efforts to restore and preserve the traditional dhows or sailing ships which are the symbol of the nation.

The Kuwaitis seem to be obsessed with the idea that not long ago--within living memory even--theirs was a poor country. There certainly was a stark contrast between the oil rich Kuwait of the mid-1980s and the bleak, dusty country portrayed in the old black-and-white photographs. These photos reveal that even the amir's palace was a very primitive structure back then. Pictures and television programs about the pre-oil era serve to demonstrate how much economic progress Kuwait has made in such a short period of time. But there also seems to be a sense of nostalgia in this fascination with the past. The television programs in particular convey a sense that while Kuwaitis were previously poor and relatively unknown, they were also a self-reliant nation which could overcome adversity. Oil brought Kuwaitis wealth and fame, but it also seems to have taken away their self-reliance.

* * *

Before my visit to the country, I had sometimes heard people refer to the Kuwaitis as the "cocktail party liberals" of the Gulf: despite the fact that Kuwait was ruled by a traditional monarchy, Kuwaitis were vocal advocates of all sorts of leftist causes in international relations, and were vociferously critical of American foreign policy. My meeting with a group of professors at Kuwait University showed me that this reputation was well deserved.

Although much of the faculty at Kuwait University come from other Arab countries, the group I met happened to be all Kuwaiti. I was describing to them my meetings with several senior Saudi officials when one of the Kuwaiti professors interrupted by saying that if I wanted to learn about Saudi foreign policy, I should not have spoken to any Saudis at all but stayed in Washington since, "Saudi Arabia is completely controlled by the United States." The others agreed heartily with this.

I asked how it was that he came to this conclusion. He said the explanation was very simple. The Saudi government agreed and cooperated with the United States on a whole host of issues. But because of American support for Israel, no self-respecting Arab government would voluntarily collaborate with the U.S. to such an extent. The fact that the Saudi government did so not only "proved" that it must not be acting voluntarily, but that it "had to be" controlled by Washington.

I suggested an alternate theory: despite their differences with Washington over Israel, the Saudi leadership understood that Israel was not a threat to their very existence the way various radical regimes in neighboring Arab states, Iran, or the Soviet Union were. Thus, the Saudis saw it as being very much in their interests to maintain a close alliance with the U.S.

The Kuwaiti professors dismissed this explanation out of hand; it was "obviously" false. I then asked them to provide the "proof" that the U.S. controlled Saudi Arabia. "But the way Saudi Arabia acts is proof in itself," was the response. They all nodded knowingly at this.

I wondered whether the Kuwaiti students were learning anything of value if this was the kind of circular logic which their professors taught. But then, I supposed it didn't matter what they learned: they were all likely to get high-paid, low-demand jobs in the civil service or the state-controlled economic sector anyway.

* * *

An Egyptian I had known in Washington had recently moved with his wife to Kuwait. I had phoned him from Washington when I was first planning my visit; he immediately invited me to stay with them. I called him a few weeks before leaving Washington to tell him the exact dates I would be in Kuwait and make sure that he could put me up. "I'm so sorry," he said, "but my cousin and his wife will be staying with us then. But do call me when you arrive so we can get together."

I called him at his office the morning after I arrived. We agreed that he would pick me up at my hotel that evening on his way home from work. We would then go meet his wife and have dinner. It occurred to me later that day that he had made no mention of his cousin.

When we met that evening, the first thing he said after we greeted each other was, "I'm sorry that you couldn't stay with us. After the two embassies were bombed last December, a decree was issued forbidding non-Kuwaitis from letting any visitors except close relatives stay overnight in their homes. I was afraid to tell you that over the phone in case it was bugged, so I made up the story about my cousin and his wife."

Thus begun my introduction to life in Kuwait from the viewpoint of non-Kuwaiti Arabs. He later told me that he and most non-Kuwaitis he knew drove more cautiously here than the Kuwaitis. For whenever there was an automobile accident involving a Kuwaiti and a non-Kuwaiti, the first thing that happened was that the non-Kuwaiti was taken to jail even if the accident was not his fault.

At the restaurant where we ate dinner, my friend, his wife, and their two friends (who were Palestinian) complained bitterly that all Kuwaitis viewed all non-Kuwaitis in their country as servants. This made working with them very difficult. Kuwaitis were always the office directors. That was to be expected. But what really annoyed them was that Kuwaitis who were officially their subordinates or juniors in the office did not behave as such. Not only did they not follow orders from more senior non-Kuwaitis (who, my friends admitted, were usually too fearful to issue any), but they never felt shy about giving orders to them. No matter how educated and experienced a non-Kuwaiti was, at work he was at the beck and call of any Kuwaiti no matter how uneducated or inexperienced. And to hear them tell it, most Kuwaitis were nothing but uneducated and inexperienced.

My friend's wife was especially bitter. She taught English to Kuwaiti schoolgirls. Maintaining discipline in the classroom was very difficult for her, she complained. For both she and her students knew that ultimately a non-Kuwaiti teacher could not penalize Kuwaiti students in any serious way: if a Kuwaiti student complained about a non-Kuwaiti teacher, that teacher would probably lose her job and be forced to leave the country.

What seemed to bother my four friends more than anything else, though, was not how Kuwaitis treated all non-Kuwaitis, but how they treated non-Kuwaiti Arabs in particular. Behind this appeared to be a strong conviction that the wealth enjoyed by the Kuwaitis was not legitimately theirs. The riches of Kuwait, Saudi Arabia, and the other Arab Gulf monarchies were seen by them as the property of all Arabs, not just the few who happened to live in a group of states which had only been created recently, and mainly as a result of British imperialism.

* * *

Despite what these four and many other non-Kuwaiti Arabs told me about the unfair treatment they received at the hands of the Kuwaitis, I did not feel especially sorry for them. If the Kuwaitis had not admitted them in large numbers to their country, these non-Kuwaiti Arabs would not be working in the relatively high paying jobs here which were unavailable in the poor countries they came from. And while the Kuwaiti government could not be mistaken for a democracy, its rule was far more benign than the regimes in those poorer Arab states. The Palestinians especially, I thought, had no right to complain about Kuwait since they were treated far better here than in Israeli occupied Arab territory or in the refugee camps that other Arab states forced them to live in. And if all non-Kuwaiti Arabs thought about Kuwait in the way that the ones I met did, then it was no wonder the Kuwaitis (who were outnumbered by foreigners in their own country) were suspicious and took measures to keep them under control.

Thus, despite the many complaints against them which I heard made by non-Kuwaiti Arabs, I sympathized with the Kuwaitis--until I found myself to be the victim of Kuwaiti disdain for non-Kuwaitis. It happened at the airport on my way out. I had been in a long check-in line for the British Airways flight to London. After waiting for some time, I was finally at the head of the line when suddenly an Arab woman came and stood in front of me. "Excuse me," I said to her, "but there is a line here."

"I am a Kuwaiti," she replied, barely deigning to turn her head toward me for a second. I was about to launch into a tirade about how she had to wait in line like everybody else when the person in back of me tapped me on the shoulder.

"Don't say anything," an elderly Englishman said quietly. "You won't get her to move and you will only cause trouble for yourself."

Hearing this just made me angrier. But I looked at the faces of the people behind him. All of them had seen the woman cut in front of me; she had really cut in front of all of us. Yet it was clear that none of them was going to say anything to her either.

I swallowed my pride, turned back around, and stared angrily at the woman's back. She never looked at me, but went up to a ticket counter when the next agent was free. Everyone behaved as if nothing out of the ordinary had occurred. Indeed, for everyone except me, nothing had.

It was a small injustice, but it suddenly made me sympathize with the non-Kuwaiti Arabs. And while this was one small indignity that happened to me just as I was leaving, I realized that non-Kuwaitis living there probably experienced worse injustices repeatedly.

When Saddam Hussein invaded Kuwait in 1990, the Western media gave a lot of coverage to how Arabs in the poorer Middle Eastern countries supported him. But I think these people were far more anti-Kuwaiti than they were pro-Iraqi. And as much as I might deplore the sentiment, I could fully understand the sense of triumph which poorer Arabs felt about how, after having humiliated so many non-Kuwaiti Arabs for so many years, the Kuwaitis were finally humiliated themselves.

In the Land of Saddam

The first thing he said to me when I met him in person was, "So when are you coming to Iraq?"

The speaker was Nizar Hamdoon. When we met in the summer of 1984, he was head of the Iraqi interests section in Washington. The following year, he would become Iraq's ambassador to Washington when the U.S. and Iraq formally re-established their diplomatic relations which had been broken since the 1967 Arab-Israeli war. Later still, he would return to Baghdad as a deputy foreign minister. After the war over Kuwait, he would be sent back to the U.S. as Iraq's ambassador to the United Nations.

While we all know how awful Saddam Hussein is now, Washington did not see him that way during the mid-1980s. This was partly due to the fear of what would happen in the region if Iranian forces defeated Iraq. But back then, Saddam was not just seen as less worse than the Ayatollah Khomeini. He actually had a positive image in Washington. And probably more than anyone else, the person responsible for creating that positive image of Saddam was Nizar Hamdoon.

Hamdoon actively argued the case that America should support Iraq in the war against Iran. Unlike most Arab diplomats, Hamdoon sought out pro-Israelis in Washington. His argument was quite simple: if Iraq was defeated, only weak little Jordan lay in the path of an Iranian advance toward Israel itself. American support for Iraq, then, was actually American support for Israel. It was an argument that persuaded many people--only too well, it turned out.

What was also remarkable about Hamdoon was that he sought contact not just with high level policy-makers in Washington, but with everyone. He went all over the U.S., visiting college and even high school campuses to make his pitch. Most remarkable of all, he sought out those who argued against American support to Iraq in order to persuade them that they were wrong. And he often succeeded.

If someone wrote or publicly said anything about Iraq, Nizar Hamdoon would be in touch. That's why I was meeting him for lunch now. The very day after I published an op-ed piece about the Iran-Iraq war in *The Christian Science Monitor*, he called me up saying he wanted to talk with me.

We met at one of Washington's typical "power lunch" restaurants where the decor is lovely, the food is good but not excellent, and the service is poor. There seems to be some kind of unwritten code: the more expensive a French restaurant is, the ruder its waiters are. Maybe they think that if they are helpful, the Washington elite would not consider the establishment to be exclusive enough, and thus would not come there any more.

Hamdoon displayed his legendary intelligence and urbanity during lunch. He made his pitch about why America should support Iraq. But he was not dogmatic. Indeed, he even acknowledged that Baghdad had made some "mistakes" in the past. But it was now abandoning its radical stance and adopting a moderate one, he assured me. His knowledge of the Washington scene was also highly impressive. If Hamdoon was a typical example of an Iraqi official, I thought, it would definitely be worthwhile for me to go to Baghdad and meet with others like him.

Thus, in answer to his question about when I would visit Iraq, I told him that I was ready to go whenever he could get permission from Baghdad. But remembering how it took over a year for me to get permission from Riyadh to visit Saudi Arabia, I did not think I would hear anything further from the Iraqis for months--if at all. However, it was only a matter of weeks before one of Hamdoon's assistants called to inform me that permission had been granted; all that remained was for me to tell them my travel plans.

* * *

I decided to make the trip just after Christmas, 1984. A few weeks ahead of time, I went over to the Iraqi interests section to get my visa and meet with Hamdoon before leaving.

"When you get to Baghdad," he said, "you will be met by someone from the Information Ministry. Although we proposed your trip through the Foreign Ministry, the Information Ministry is responsible for hosting foreign scholars such as yourself."

My heart sank. I recounted how when the Saudi embassy arranged for me to visit Riyadh eight months previously, the Information Ministry there had been my host. I had been told that the Information Ministry would plan everything and would even meet me at the airport. But when I arrived, there had been no one from the ministry to meet me. Nor had the ministry made a single appointment for me in advance.

Hamdoon laughed. "We are not like them," he assured me. "We Iraqis are efficient. You will be met at the airport, and your appointments will all be arranged."

I asked if he could tell me which hotel I was booked into just in case no one was there to meet me and I had to get to it on my own.

He didn't know where I'd be staying, he responded. "Don't worry: nothing like that could happen in Iraq."

* * *

But it did. When I arrived in Baghdad late at night, there was no one from the Iraqi Information Ministry waiting for me. Fortunately for me, however, someone else was.

I had told a friend of mine at the State Department in Washington that I would be going to Iraq. He insisted on notifying the U.S. interests section there "just in case." The grim-faced American diplomat who greeted me said that the U.S. interests section in Baghdad usually sent someone to the airport to greet any Americans arriving under the Information Ministry's auspices since it routinely failed to meet its guests.

"There isn't very good communication between the Iraqi interests section in Washington and the Information Ministry here." This was going to be a rerun of my visit to Saudi Arabia. Well, if the Iraqi Information Ministry was going to provide me with as little help as the Saudi one, I would thwart it by calling Hamdoon back in Washington and make my appointments through him just as I had through the Saudi embassy on my earlier trip.

"Do you know where you are staying?" asked the diplomat.

"No."

"That's also typical. We've made a reservation for you at a hotel. I'll take you there now."

The drive into town surprised me somewhat. This was the first time I had visited a country at war. In fact, the front was only about one hundred miles to the east of Baghdad. Yet despite the fact that it had frequently been attacked from the air by the Iranians, the city was completely lit up. I had thought that nations at war imposed blackouts. That, anyway, was what happened in all the World War II movies I had watched when I was a kid.

When I asked about this, the diplomat replied, "Iraq and Iran bombard each other, but usually with missiles, not aircraft. The missiles they each have aren't very accurate, but what little accuracy they have doesn't depend on whether it is light or dark. So the lights are kept on."

I was dropped off at the Palestine Meridien--which was not, I would soon discover, the flagship of the French hotel chain it belonged to. The diplomat advised me to call Hamdoon immediately while his office was still open back in Washington. Since tomorrow was Friday--the Muslim holy day--he doubted that the Information Ministry would contact me then. If I hadn't heard from anyone there by Saturday morning, I should take a cab down to the U.S. interests section and they would help straighten things out for me.

As soon as I checked in and went up to my room, I phoned Hamdoon's office in Washington. It was still open, but I was told that Hamdoon was out of town for a couple of weeks. His assistant said he would send a cable to inform Baghdad of my arrival, but also said that neither he nor anyone else there could do anything to help arrange appointments for me (they did not have Hamdoon's clout). "But when the Information Ministry gets in touch with you, it will arrange everything. Don't worry."

This was not good news. Still, if the Iraqi interests section in Washington would not help me, perhaps the U.S. interests section here in Baghdad could. The fact that it had sent someone to pick me up at the airport demonstrated that the diplomats there were friendly. I would be sure to go over there on Saturday whether or not I had heard from the Information Ministry by then.

* * *

I slept late Friday after my long flights from Washington to Frankfurt and then from Frankfurt to Baghdad. I didn't wake up until about noon. It was then that I looked around my room. There was a view of the Tigris River out my window. But the room itself smelled like gas. I switched on the television. There was an in-house channel which showed Western movies. Even though it was in-house, the image on the screen was poor. But the regular television channels came in clearly. There was even some programming in English. No matter what time I tuned in, Saddam Hussein was usually on the set. He was being cheered everywhere he went.

Outside my door was a copy of the English language Iraqi newspaper, *The Baghdad Observer*. The entire second page in this and all subsequent editions I read was devoted to reprinting extracts from the last congress of the ruling Ba'th party. It was all about striving to fulfill the goals of the revolution and adhering to the line set down by the Revolutionary Command Council, especially its heroic chairman Saddam Hussein.

In this and subsequent editions, there was also news about the war with

Iran. Each day there was a story about an Iranian missile attack. There was something unusual about these attacks: according to the paper, the Iranian missiles only seemed to hit hospitals, elementary schools, or private homes-- nothing else. Funny. There was also plenty about the doings of Saddam, the messages he received from the leaders of other countries, and the messages he sent out. As in most Arab countries, the contents of the messages were never disclosed; only the bare facts of who they had been received from or sent to.

Similar non-stories filled the rest of the paper. Although I didn't learn much from it, reading *The Baghdad Observer* definitely helped me fall asleep each night.

* * *

By mid-morning on Saturday, no one had called from the Information Ministry or anywhere else, so I took a cab from the hotel to the U.S. interests section. This cab ride was my first opportunity to get a good look at Baghdad by day.

There was not the grinding poverty here that I had seen in Cairo. On the other hand, Baghdad did not seem like a prosperous city either--although it should have been considering Iraq's enormous oil wealth. Men and women wore mainly Western style clothes instead of traditional Arab dress.

There were soldiers everywhere. Most seemed to be in transit--riding in buses, trucks, vans, or simply walking in groups. They appeared to be exhausted.

There were others, however, who were wide awake. These were soldiers with automatic rifles guarding virtually every government building and major intersection. As the taxi approached each of these places, the soldiers pointed their rifles directly at us. As we moved past, they redirected them toward other oncoming vehicles.

We were not allowed to stop closer than almost a block away from the U.S. interests section. There must have been a dozen soldiers there. One of them asked to see my passport. He nodded that I could go in, but each soldier I walked past had his rifle aimed at me.

Once I gained admittance, the diplomat who picked me up at the airport introduced me to most of the very small staff there. While one person set about calling various people at the Information Ministry in the hope that someone there would recognize my name, the head of the interests section briefed me on the current situation in Iraq. I asked him if he could help me make some appointments since I did not expect much help from the

Information Ministry.

"We have a hard time getting in to see people ourselves. It just wouldn't work if we tried to set anything up for you. Most people would be too afraid to meet you if we tried to arrange a meeting; they risk being seen as spies by the security services. Also, if Iraqis know you are the guest of the Information Ministry, no one would dare offend it by meeting you outside its auspices."

Just then, someone came in to say that an official at the Information Ministry had been found who recognized my name. "He volunteered to send a car over for you, but we said you'd go over in one of ours. Knowing them, it might be hours before their car gets here."

Just as I was saying good-bye, the office head told me that I should come down and brief them about meetings I had with high level officials if the Information Ministry actually did arrange any. But from the tone of his voice, it was clear he thought this was not likely.

* * *

When I arrived at the Information Ministry, I walked very slowly past all the soldiers pointing their rifles at me. I presented myself at the reception desk, and someone took me to a large office where two men who looked like thugs were sitting behind a single desk. "Welcome to Iraq," they each said in an unwelcoming voice as I shook hands with them.

"We knew you were coming in Thursday night," one of them said, "but we thought you would be on the flight from London, not from Frankfurt. We waited for you after the London flight arrived, but we thought you must not have come." There seemed to be a note of disappointment that I had come after all.

I soon learned that, despite what Hamdoon had told me, absolutely no appointments had been arranged for me. They asked me what I was interested in and who I wanted to see. I told them about my research and asked for meetings at the Foreign Ministry, the Defense Ministry, and the president's office.

"This will be difficult," said the other. "We will send telexes to these various offices to tell them about you. It might be awhile before they respond."

I then suggested, rather helpfully I thought, that it might be more efficient if they made telephone calls instead of sending telexes.

"That is not our procedure," was the flat response.

"Considering the length of time it might take to get responses," I said, "it is a pity that you didn't send out the telexes before I arrived."

"That also is not our procedure. What if we had sent out telexes for you but you did not arrive?" Send out more telexes was the thought that immediately sprang to my mind, but I guessed that that too was not their procedure.

I decided not to press the issue; there was no point in getting into an argument. With no help from the Iraqi interests section in Washington or the U.S. interests section here, I realized that I was totally dependent on the Information Ministry for whatever program it deigned to arrange for me.

"Don't worry," said one of the thugs. "We will arrange excellent program for you. But today, we will have someone take you back to your hotel so you can rest."

I wasn't tired right then, but I was after waiting an additional hour and a half for the ministry's car and driver to show up.

* * *

On the way back to the hotel, we drove along a road where there were two large signs warning cars to "Slow Down" and "Reduce Speed Now" in English as well as Arabic. But instead of slowing down, every car--including my own--speeded up as we drove past an enormous fenced-in compound.

I asked my driver what was inside the compound. He responded with one word: *"mukhabarat."* This was one of the dreaded security services. Just then, we passed a guard tower in which several soldiers were sitting behind machine guns pointed at us. Beyond this was a portrait of Saddam which was at least three stories tall.

Once we had gotten beyond the *mukhabarat's* compound, traffic slowed down again.

* * *

Baghdad didn't strike me as the kind of place where foreigners sightseeing on their own would be welcome. So I spent the rest of the day in my hotel room. I watched a few of the less-than-Oscar category Western movies on the in-house channel. I switched to the regular channel occasionally in order to keep up with Saddam's doings. I had brought one fat, nine hundred page novel with me from home. When I left Washington, I thought that this would be more than enough to keep me occupied during any free time on my trip. I now feared that I would finish it too soon and would only have *The*

Baghdad Observer to read.

I woke up at six a.m. the next morning, hopeful that the Information Ministry had spent the previous day arranging a busy program for me. I ordered breakfast to be delivered to my room for fear that I would miss any phone calls. But I waited in vain for hours.

I had given up hope and was just about to call room service and order lunch when the phone rang. "Hello," I said eagerly.

A terse, unfriendly voice stated, "This is Samir from the Information Ministry. I am in the lobby waiting for you."

"I'll be right down," I responded.

Three minutes later, I was shaking hands with a short, unsmiling man. "Come with me," he said abruptly. "We have program for you." Something told me that being my guide was not an assignment he had volunteered for.

"Where are we going?" I asked.

"You will see," was his response.

There were several limousines and Mercedes Benzes waiting in the hotel driveway. None of these, however, was for us. Samir led me to a very small Brazilian-made car. The seal of the Information Ministry was painted on the front door as were the Iraqi and PLO flags.

Samir ushered me into the extremely cramped back seat while he sat up front with the driver. The first time the driver braked suddenly, I realized that the seat I was sitting on was not attached to its frame. Unfortunately for me, this particular driver often braked suddenly, and so I was forced to ride with one hand on the back of the front seat in order to avoid being thrown against it.

When we came to a sudden stop, it took me a moment to realize that we had not narrowly avoided a collision, but had parked. "We are here," said Samir informatively.

We had arrived at one of the enormous Arab socialist realist monuments that are scattered all over Baghdad. This one, Samir told me, was the monument to the unknown soldier. In the midst of a large open space, a huge oval extended at an approximately forty-five degree angle into the sky.

I started to take a photograph of this with my camera. "Only take pictures after asking permission," Samir intoned, somewhat menacingly.

"Can I take a picture of the monument?" I asked.

"Yes," he answered in his usual monotone. So I did.

I asked Samir what the oval symbolized. "A palm tree," he replied curtly.

We walked in silence up a slight incline to the oval. There was a good view of the surrounding city from the oval. "This is where Saddam speaks with the masses," said Samir. This statement shocked me somewhat, not because of its content, but that Samir had volunteered it without being asked a question first.

"Let us go down below," he said next. He really was becoming talkative. I soon learned that beneath the oval was a museum of sorts. The theme of the exhibit was "the struggle of the Iraqi people against imperialism." There were displays featuring Iraq's internal and external conflicts during the twentieth century. Among these were the Iraqi role in the 1967 and 1973 Arab-Israeli wars, the 1958 overthrow of the Iraqi monarchy, various uprisings against the British during the inter-war years, and, of course, the war against Iran. The displays showed the various types of uniform worn by Iraqi servicemen and the kinds of weapons they employed against their opponents--including pistols, rifles, and more sophisticated weaponry.

My favorite display was a small one about resistance to the imposition of the British mandate in Iraq following the end of World War I and the breakup of the Ottoman Empire. There were hardly any weapons in the display case, but one of them was a pitch fork. Samir noticed me lingering over this. He came over and said, "We lost this struggle because we had such poor weapons."

On the walls of the room were plaques presented by the military attaches or visiting delegations from mainly Arab and communist countries. In the center of the museum was an extraordinary display. Suspended from the ceiling was a series of hearts in a spiral pattern. In Iraq (and perhaps elsewhere), the representation of the human heart is upside-down from the common Western version: the rounded parts are on the bottom and the point is on the top. Through each of these hearts was thrust a sword. "This symbolizes how the Iraqi people deal with their enemies," Samir told me.

* * *

The next stop was the monument to the "martyrs," meaning specifically all those who had died in the ongoing war against Iran. In the midst of yet another immense space was an enormous pair of heart-shaped half domes. The two domes together represented a heart. Their being split and set apart from each other was meant to symbolize a broken heart. Oddly enough, the outer part of the gigantic split heart was painted turquoise.

"You may take a picture," Samir informed me. So I did. This began a pattern: instead of me asking to take pictures when I wanted to, I would take them whenever he announced out of the blue that I could do so.

As we approached the monument, it became clear that it was a lot larger-- and a lot farther away--than I had originally thought. When we finally reached it, there was another underground museum to visit. The exhibit in this one featured the life of Saddam Hussein before he came to power. The various displays showed what a stalwart revolutionary he had been ever since boyhood. And, of course, he had been very studious: there was one of his report cards showing that he had received all top grades.

One display discussed two trips Saddam made outside Iraq before coming to power. The first was to Nasser's Egypt, and the second was to Syria. Apparently these were the only two foreign trips he ever took before undertaking his "glorious task." His knowledge of countries outside the Arab world, then, was limited to the anti-Western rhetoric of Ba`th party ideology.

Despite the extensive nature of the exhibit, I could not get a sense of how Saddam's personality developed in his early years. Everything that was depicted was painted in glowing, heroic, and hence completely hollow terms.

More interesting than observing the displays was observing the other visitors. These were mostly school children who were being led around in groups by guides. The guides were addressing their young charges in taut, emotional voices. The children would occasionally clap simultaneously, but for the most part did not look very happy. Samir didn't either; I guess he'd seen it all before. We didn't stay very long.

* * *

I asked Samir where we were going next. "Baghdad Museum," he replied curtly as we walked back toward our little Brazilian car. I told him that I had really hoped to meet with people at the Foreign and Defense Ministries. This, after all, was why I had come to Baghdad--not to play tourist.

"You must have cultural program first," Samir responded. "It is important for all visitors to understand Iraqi culture."

I wanted to tell him that I thought he was right, but that so far I had learned less about culture than the cult of personality. I didn't think Samir would appreciate me saying so, however. So I tried a different approach. "I want to visit a mosque," I announced.

Samir stopped in his tracks. "A mosque?" he asked incredulously. "Why?"

"Because Islam is an important part of Iraqi culture."

He obviously couldn't argue with that. He shook his head, but then smiled. "Maybe another day," he said. And off we went to the Baghdad Museum. Here, at least, there were some exhibits about Iraq from before the birth of Saddam.

* * *

The next morning I was waiting for Samir in the lobby when he showed up about nine. Since I had nothing else to do the previous evening, I read that fat novel I had brought along. As a result of jet lag, I had not only been unable to fall asleep, but I ended up finishing the novel. With nothing of interest left to read, I was in a state of hopelessness. I asked Samir what interviews had been arranged for me that day.

"There are no interviews today," he answered in his monotone. "Today, we have more cultural program. We go now to Babylon."

As we approached the little Brazilian car, I asked Samir how long the trip to Babylon would take. "Maybe two hours," he replied. The prospect of fighting to keep the back seat in place for two hours going and then two hours coming was not pleasant.

The reality, however, was worse than I anticipated. The Brazilian car was not air conditioned. Hence Samir and the driver rolled down their front windows. Once we were out of town, the dust from the desert all seemed to fly in through their windows and behind my contact lenses. When I asked them to roll their windows up, they did so, but soon rolled them back down again as the temperature inside the car quickly rose.

From what I could see when I wasn't rubbing my eyes, the standard of living seemed to fall off dramatically outside of Baghdad. The small towns and villages we drove through consisted of mostly one- or two-story buildings, all of which were poorly constructed. Yet while they may not have had much else, all these little places had an abundance of Iraqi flags and portraits of Saddam.

* * *

Something more must be said about these portraits. Although the ruler's picture is posted throughout other Arab countries I have visited, in none of them is it as ever present as that of Saddam Hussein in Iraq. Saddam's face is literally everywhere there. On the streets, his pictures are frequently only a few feet apart from one another. Inside one government building, I saw an office where there were pictures of Saddam Hussein on the desk and on all four walls as well.

Like the ninety-nine names of Allah that proclaim all His various attributes, there are at least as many types of portrait of Saddam displaying the various sides of his personality. Among them are Saddam in civilian clothes, Saddam with Arab headdress, Saddam in fatigues, Saddam in dress uniform, Saddam brandishing various types of weapons, Saddam comforting widows and orphans, and Saddam with the masses. All of these come in two variations: Saddam with and without dark glasses.

My favorite one, though, requires some explaining. Outside Baghdad is Cteisophon, where Samir took me on another occasion. Cteisophon was the old Persian capital where in the seventh century A.D., an Arab army defeated a much larger Persian army, forcing the Persians to abandon the city and retreat to the east. The ruins of Cteisophon are a majestic site, and there were many people there viewing them with me.

Less than majestic, though, is a round structure nearby where on the inside twenty-four North Korean "artists" had drawn a mural depicting the ancient battle between Arabs and Persians. The Arabs are all in white and the Persians are all in blue; the latter are shown being slain in particularly graphic ways with blood gushing forth from their bodies.

On the road to the Baghdad airport (named, not surprisingly, Saddam International Airport), there is a large billboard with a scene from this mural showing the Arabs on horseback charging with their spears. Beside them is Saddam Hussein wearing fatigues and cheering them on.

* * *

The Babylon excavation site encompassed a large area. Only one of the buildings, however, had been fully "restored." This was the main gate into Babylon. The building was painted dark blue with gold trim. The images of various animals carved into the bricks were alternately painted white and gold. The main gate had two turrets which looked more like they belonged on a medieval English castle than in Babylon. It struck me that the building I was looking at may have been less an accurate representation of the original than an act of historical imagination.

While this one building seemed over-restored, the rest of the site had received considerably less attention. It was really a small city, with several large buildings, lots of small ones, and a few public areas. The site was not marked to prevent visitors from walking anywhere they pleased. There was rubble and trash everywhere, especially around the smaller buildings. With the war going on, restoring Babylon was apparently not a high priority.

I thought that the Iraqis could have developed a tourist industry like the Egyptians had. This would feature visits to the ancient sites of Mesopotamia and cruises along the Tigris and Euphrates. Of course, to do this successfully would require the Iraqi government to treat foreigners with a modicum of civility and deference in order to attract large numbers of them. I doubted that the regime of Saddam Hussein could accomplish this.

The one amenity for tourists that I saw at Babylon was a souvenir stand.

Three items were on sale: rocks with cuneiform painted on them, clay rectangles with an image of a man similar to those found in the Baghdad Museum, and maps of Iraq. I bought one of each. The map had one very surprising feature: instead of Saddam's picture on it, it had the picture of the previous president. Baghdad really must have forgotten about this place.

On the way back, Samir had the driver pull off the main highway onto a dirt road. We drove up a slight hill and stopped. There was an enormous pit. We got out. "Here is where they find the Tower of Babel," said Samir.

"So where is it?" I asked.

"Have to dig more," Samir replied. A more accurate reply would have been, "Have to build it."

We drove back to Baghdad. As I was getting out of the car at my hotel, Samir said, "Tomorrow is New Year's Day. Many government officials Christian, so they won't work. We have no interviews tomorrow."

Seeing my disappointment, Samir added, "But maybe I will come by. We will have more cultural program." I thanked him and proceeded sadly up to my room.

* * *

Being by myself in my room on New Year's Eve became increasingly lonely as the night wore on, especially after I finished reading every word of that day's *Baghdad Observer*.

Ever since I had arrived at this hotel, I had noticed signs in the lobby announcing not one, but two New Year's Eve parties. Admission to one was about fifty dollars per person, while admission to the other was about one hundred dollars. I had decided not to attend: although being alone by oneself can sometimes be lonely, being alone in a crowd is always so.

Just to get out of my room, at about ten p.m. I went and sat in the lobby to see how many and what kind of people came to the New Year's Eve parties.

A steady stream of party-goers was coming through the hotel entrance. Almost all were Arabs, and probably Iraqis. They seemed to be coming in groups, most of which seemed to consist of an older couple (probably a husband and wife) accompanied by young women (their daughters). There were almost no young men. These, I presumed, were off fighting the war.

Everyone seemed to be dressed quite elegantly, with the men in suits or tuxedos and the women in long evening gowns and wearing lots of jewelry. These people were definitely not poor. I wondered who they might be. Businessmen? High level bureaucrats? Whoever they were, this was the only occasion when I observed large numbers of Iraqis laughing, smiling, and enjoying themselves.

At about 11:45 p.m., I decided to go back up to my room. I turned on the local English language radio station and listened to the announcer's long tribute to Saddam which began just after midnight. She waxed eloquent about his many virtues, including his wisdom, bravery, compassion, etc. After fifteen minutes, I switched the radio off. I wondered just how much longer she would go on. Her voice sounded as if she believed what she was saying. Of course, she wouldn't have kept the job long if it did not.

* * *

The next morning when Samir came to the hotel, he was alone. For once, I was able to sit in the front seat of the car, which was firmly anchored down.

"You wanted to go to a mosque," he said. "I will take you to one."

Samir drove even more rapidly than the usual driver. Once we parked, we had to walk a long way before we entered the grounds of the mosque. It was beautiful. The building was very large and had gold turrets and what looked like elaborate chandeliers hanging in the entry ways.

"This is the main Shia mosque," said Samir a little nervously. "We should not get too close to it."

It is well known that most Iranians belong to the Shia branch of Islam and most Arabs to the Sunni branch. Yet while Iraq is a predominantly Arab country, it is believed that the majority of the population there are also Shia. To the extent that they can be said to adhere to any religion, Saddam Hussein and his government come from the Sunni Arab minority.

The fierce stares we received from the men in the vicinity indicated that our presence was not welcome. Samir seemed nervous. I took several photographs of the mosque. Only later did it occur to me that I had not asked Samir whether this was permitted, nor had he said I could. Sensing that Samir was off balance here, I walked toward one side of the building and he followed. I walked straight up to the building and photographed it. I started to walk around toward the entrance when Samir finally asserted himself. "We must go," he said.

We went back to the car. After driving along for awhile, Samir suddenly pulled into a parking lot. "This is a hard currency store," he informed me. "I want you to buy me a bottle of whiskey with dollars. I will pay you back in dinars."

I suddenly understood. Taking me to the mosque--which I had asked to see--was not part of the official tour. He had taken me there on his own, without the regular driver to observe, as a favor. And he had done this in the expectation that I would return the favor by helping him buy the whiskey which he could not get with Iraqi currency.

I said I would do it. We went together into the hard currency store. It was a pretty dreary place. When I had visited the Soviet Union the year before, there was not much available in the ordinary stores that Russians shopped at, but at least the hard currency stores for the foreigners were fairly well stocked. Here, however, there was an extremely limited selection. I had never heard of any of the few brands of alcohol on sale. Samir pointed to the kind he wanted. I bought the bottle for fifteen dollars. Back in the car, we exchanged whiskey for dinars. "Thanks," he said, actually smiling.

When we got back to my hotel, I invited him to have lunch with me. In the coffee shop, we sat mainly in silence. But out of the blue, he asked me, "What do you think of the situation in East Germany?"

"I think it is pretty terrible," I replied, startled by his question. "It is one of the mostly tightly controlled communist states."

"Have you ever been there?" he asked.

I admitted that I had not.

"Then I think what you say is just Western propaganda," he remarked.

"Why do you say that?" I asked.

"Because I went with an Iraqi delegation to East Germany. It seemed just fine to me."

Compared to Iraq, it probably was.

After lunch, I walked with him back outside to where his car was parked. "It's getting cloudy," I noted.

"Yes," he responded, "just like the mood of the Iraqi people."

I was surprised to hear him utter what could be construed as anti-government sentiments. I asked him to explain what he meant. Instead of answering, he got in his car and drove away.

* * *

On Wednesday and Thursday--my last two full days in Iraq--I finally got my interviews. They were not quite what I had hoped for, but they were revealing in their own way.

I had asked for appointments at the Foreign Ministry, but I ended up getting one at the Foreign Trade Ministry instead. My primary interest in coming to Iraq was to enquire about the politico-military aspects of the Soviet-Iraqi relationship. All I could think to ask the Foreign Trade Ministry official was whether Soviet-Iraqi trade was rising or falling.

Apparently seeing this question as an affront, the official responded, "Our great leader, Saddam Hussein has said, `Iraq welcomes foreign trade with all nations!' This answers your question fully!"

I would not have realized it unless he had said so. I posed a few other questions about the overall Soviet-Iraqi trade balance, what each side bought from and sold to the other, and the level of Iraqi debt to Moscow. Each time, all I got in return was a quote from Saddam and advice that what he had said made everything "crystal clear."

After the fourth or fifth repetition of this line, I thanked the official for his time and said I shouldn't take up any more of it. For his part, he did not seem sad to see me go. I couldn't help wondering why he had met me to begin with. Perhaps this was still part of the "cultural program."

* * *

The saddest experience was visiting Baghdad University. Samir took me to see the chair of the social sciences faculty. He made a few calls and soon there were eight professors in the office, plus Samir and me. We had a very animated discussion about various issues. Unlike most Arab universities I had visited, the professors here were not rabidly anti-American. Several of them had received Ph.D.s at American universities--all before Saddam came to power. One had received his degree in the Soviet Union; he seemed the most pro-American of all. Each of them indicated how much they would love to be invited to a conference in the U.S. or, better yet, to teach in the U.S. for a semester or a year. Each gave me his or her card.

We talked for nearly an hour and a half. The session came to an end when Samir, who had said nothing up to now, looked at his watch and announced that we had to go. The chair made a little speech praising the Information Ministry for having brought me there.

"Where are we going now?" I asked Samir as we were walking toward the car.

He looked blankly at me. "Nowhere at the moment," he said. He had apparently gotten bored during my conversation with the professors. He could have, I thought, left and come back for me later. But either this never occurred to him or leaving the professors with me without a chaperone from the Information Ministry was not permitted.

* * *

I was taken to see the head of some publishing house. Samir did not come into the office with me for this interview. Perhaps because the publishing house was part of the Information Ministry, a chaperone from the same ministry was not necessary.

I was given a long harangue about how the ongoing war with Iran had been imposed on Iraq by Tehran. Iraq wanted peace, he told me over and over again.

"Wasn't it Iraq that started the war by invading Iran back in September 1980?" I asked.

The publisher looked at me as if I had sprouted another head. "That is a propaganda!" he told me in deeply injured tones. "It was actually Iran which invaded Iraq! Baghdad merely responded to this attack."

Soon thereafter, I announced that I could not possibly take up any more of this gentleman's precious time.

* * *

Last of all, I was taken to see Naji al-Hadithi, who was then editor of none other than *The Baghdad Observer*. Samir didn't come to this interview either. Naji certainly didn't need watching. He repeated all the main propaganda themes which I had read in his paper over the past several days: Iran had imposed the war on Iraq, Iraq wanted peace while Iran wanted war, etc. I nearly burst out laughing when he described Hafez al-Assad, the ruler of neighboring Syria and the head of that country's Ba`th party, as "a dictator."

I asked him a question about one of the many full page installments of the most recent Ba`th party program which had been running on page two of his paper every day that I had seen it.

He really looked as if he had gone into shock. "You read that?" seemed to be his unspoken question.

"I ran out of things to read," I said.

"I see," he responded, and changed the subject. I had the feeling that while he may have been required to publish Ba`th party pronouncements, they were not something he read very closely himself, or expected any of his readers to peruse either.

* * *

The next day, I woke up early to pack and get ready for the morning flight to London that I was booked on. I took all my luggage down to the lobby and checked out about half an hour before Samir said he would come by to pick me up. Samir, however, did not arrive at the appointed hour.

I did not have a phone number for him, so I had no choice but to wait.

A half hour passed. I was starting to get nervous. I definitely did not want to miss this flight.

Another half hour passed. I was really getting nervous. I just wanted to get out of this country. Since my scheduled departure was only an hour away, I decided to take a taxi to the airport.

At the airport, I checked in and got in the line of passengers which had to go through three separate metal detectors before reaching passport control. After going through the third metal detector, I calmed down. I was going to get on board the flight after all.

Finally it was my turn to hand my passport through the little slot to the guard. He looked at each page slowly. He then looked up at me and said matter-of-factly, "You cannot leave. You do not have an exit visa."

I was about to protest, when suddenly Samir appeared like the cavalry in an old Western. He slipped an official looking paper through the slot and spoke rapidly to the guard. The guard shrugged, opened my passport back up, stamped it, and returned it to me. "You can go," he said in the same tone of voice.

I shook Samir's hand gratefully. "Where were you?" I asked.

"I overslept," he explained. "Sorry." We shook hands again, said good-bye, and I proceeded to the aircraft.

I had absolutely nothing to read on the long flight. Normally, this was a situation that would have put me in a sour mood. But not this time. The closer we got to London, the happier I felt.

In a Tehran Taxi

It almost never happened this way. An invitation to participate in a conference--especially one abroad--was almost always initiated with a phone call. And usually the phone call came from a friend or acquaintance. But this invitation came by letter from someone I had never heard of. And what the letter offered seemed unbelievable.

The letter arrived in mid-1991. It was from a professor at a university in Florida inviting me to attend a conference he was helping to organize which would take place in March 1992 in Tehran. What made the letter seem so unreal was that it was so ordinary. It said that the conference organizers would provide economy class airline tickets (typical for academic conferences) as well as pay for hotel accommodations. Conference participants were being asked to write a twenty-five page paper, to be completed and turned in to the professor before we embarked for Tehran. A list of scholars from the U.S. and other countries who were also being invited was provided. The letter seemed to imply that the venue of the conference--Tehran--was not particularly special or unusual.

A few days later, there was a phone call from the Florida professor's research assistant. "Are you planning to attend?" she asked. I said I'd think about it. I got in touch with some of the others on the invitation list. A few said they would not go. Others said they would accept, but would not get on the plane if conditions seemed unsafe at the time. The invitation seemed unreal to everyone I spoke with.

When the research assistant called again, I too accepted with the proviso that if conditions seemed dangerous at the time, I would back out. That was fine with her. I didn't hear much from Florida again over the next few months, though I did meet the professor who sent me the invitation at a conference we were both attending in Miami. About ten scholars from the

U.S. and Canada had accepted, he told me.

As the date of the conference approached, I heard more and more from Florida. The research assistant called me about several matters connected with the trip: airline tickets, visa, paper abstract, and the paper itself. When there were just two weeks to go before departure, phone calls suddenly proliferated among the invitees to check who in fact was really going. I called a friend at the State Department who was one of those responsible for Iranian affairs to seek his advice. He had already received several such calls, he informed me. "Officially," he said, "we have to warn you not to go. But unofficially, we'd be very interested in hearing about your experiences if you do." Since the institute sponsoring us was linked to the Iranian Foreign Ministry, he didn't think we'd have any problems--provided, of course, we didn't do anything "foolish."

In the few days before departure, I learned that the two Iranian emigres--both frequent critics of the Islamic regime--who had at first accepted invitations to the conference decided not to attend after all. The Islamic government had a habit of inviting Iranian emigres back into the country with promises of good treatment only to arrest them or not allow them back out once they had landed, one of them told me. But this was less likely to happen to non-Iranians, she assured me.

The invitation to one scholar was withdrawn at the last moment. Although Professor Robert Freedman had been invited, the Iranians subsequently became uncomfortable about identifying him in the program as coming from Baltimore Hebrew University. Would he mind being identified as coming just from "Baltimore University?" Freedman did indeed mind, and so the invitation was canceled.

What was curious about the ten or so Americans who did go was that many either were Jewish or had Jewish last names. We speculated among ourselves as to why this was the case. Was it an attempt by the Iranians to show that despite their objections to Israel, they were not prejudiced against Jews? Or believing their own propaganda about it being the Jews who "ran America," did they think we must be important? We never did ask.

* * *

Most of the American and other Western participants met up at Charles de Gaulle airport in Paris for the flight to Tehran. It just didn't seem like we were really going to Iran. Some of us joked about there still being time to turn back before stepping on board the plane. But we all got on it. Even then, everything seemed normal. Instead of putting us on their own airline, the Iranians had booked us on Air France. Most of the passengers were Westerners. Everyone behaved as if flying to Iran was the most normal thing in the world. If there was anything unusual at all, it was that the passengers seemed to be consuming more alcohol than on other flights I had been on. We joined in with everyone else, since we knew there would be no more booze until the flight out.

But when we began our descent into Tehran airport, reality set in. An announcement was made warning that alcohol could not be taken with us off the aircraft. Shortly thereafter, it was announced that women would not be permitted to leave the aircraft unless they were wearing "proper attire." This caused a stir from the two American ladies in our group.

In front of and facing me was a seat used by one of the stewardesses for take-off and landing. The French stewardess had just strapped herself in, but had not put on any additional clothing to cover her head, arms, or legs. From behind me, Elizabeth--one of the two ladies in our group--asked me to ask the stewardess how she dressed in Tehran. When I relayed this question, the stewardess replied, "We do not get off in Tehran. We fly back to Istanbul and wear what we like there." This dismayed Elizabeth and Martha even further. They hoped that the scarves and long rain coats they were wearing would pass muster.

When we got off the plane, there were three separate points at which we had to present our passports instead of the usual one in most countries. We speculated that they must represent three different bureaucracies. One was probably the regular immigration authorities, another might be the Revolutionary Guards. We couldn't figure out which the third might be. The lines moved slowly as the examiners went carefully through everyone's passport at each separate stage.

After the third stage and before baggage claim, we were greeted by a representative from our host institution--the Institute for Political and International Studies (IPIS). He was an affable, middle aged gentleman who had us wait until our entire group had cleared the passport controls. When all of our group had finally reassembled and everyone who wanted to had changed money, our guide led us into the baggage claim area. All of our bags had already been collected in one spot. After verifying that the bags were ours, we were whisked through customs without being examined and onto a waiting bus. It was late at night and so we did not see much of the city. Traffic was heavy, but not nearly as heavy as we would see later during morning and evening rush hours.

After about an hour, we reached our hotel--the Azadi (meaning "freedom"). We were told that it had been the last modern hotel built before the Iranian revolution, until which it existed briefly as the Hyatt. Staring at us as we entered the hotel lobby was a large portrait of the deceased Ayatollah Khomeini. To the right and slightly lower than Khomeini's portrait was one of President Rafsanjani. To the left of Khomeini and on the same level as Rafsanjani was a portrait of the religious leader, Ayatollah Khamen'ei.

Over the course of my visit, I would make two observations about this set of portraits. The first was that Iran was the only Middle Eastern country I had visited where the portrait of a previous ruler was given prominence. In the Arab monarchies, it was portraits of the reigning monarch and the crown prince(s) which were common. In the Arab "republics," however, the portrait of the current president was usually the only one on display. Iranian practice more closely resembled that of the Soviet Union where the portrait of the founder of the revolutionary regime, Lenin, was given pride of place.

The second observation was that there seemed to be far fewer portraits of the leadership in Iran than in either the Arab states or the USSR. This surprised me because I had thought that revolutionary regimes in particular sought to remind their citizens who it was they should be eternally grateful to. I was told that such portraits had been more common in Iran at an earlier stage, but not any more.

At the far end of the lobby was the reception desk where we all checked in. Looking back across the lobby, we observed above the entry way a message in English which in huge letters spelled, "DOWN WITH USA." We didn't know whether the sign had been put up especially for our benefit or whether it had been there for years. In either case, it was not quite the welcome which we Americans had been hoping for.

Before going up to our rooms, we were shown a table near the front of the lobby. This would be manned by the IPIS staff to help facilitate our visit, we were told. We then had to wait for the extremely slow elevator cars which served this tall building. While we were waiting, one of the Westerners stated, "Let's go for a beer!" The Westerners laughed but the Iranians did not.

One of the Iranians then said, "If you say that again, we'll take you to jail." This time the Iranians laughed but the Westerners did not.

* * *

The next morning, I was woken up by the telephone. The person on the other end told me that all the other conference participants were in the lobby ready to go on a bus tour to the Tehran bazaar. Everyone was waiting for me. I said that since I was still in bed, they had better go on without me--

which they did. My fellow conference participants would later tease me about my traveling all the way to Tehran just to sleep in.

After the phone call, I couldn't go back to sleep. It was already mid-morning anyway. I looked around the room more carefully than I had been able to do when I first entered it in an exhausted state the previous evening. I suspected that the furnishings in the room were the original ones that had been installed in the late 1970s. Some of the information cards in the room still bore the Hyatt label. Everything seemed old and shabby. Even the floor felt lumpy and uneven.

Three of my Iranian students back home had given me the names and phone numbers of some of their relatives whom they suggested I try to contact. This process took far longer than I anticipated because the telephone proved very difficult to use. To begin with, it was an old rotary dial phone. Like hotels everywhere, it was necessary to dial "9" to get an outside line. Unlike most hotels, however, this only worked about a third of the time. When I did get an outside line, I would then dial the number. Often, however, I could not even dial the entire number before being interrupted by a busy signal. On the other hand, sometimes when I did succeed in dialing the entire number, there would be no sound at all on the other end. Each time one of these problems occurred, of course, I had to start the process all over again.

Sometimes, I would actually get through to someone, but the connection was so poor that I could just barely hear the person on the other end. Even if the connection was good, there was the language barrier. After literally four hours, I finally did get through to a number of people who spoke some English. Some took my number and said that relatives more conversant in English would call me back later. A few even made tentative arrangements to meet with me. One lady told me that her husband and son would come to the hotel on Tuesday evening (today was Sunday) to pick me up and take me to their home for dinner.

Telephone service is notoriously poor throughout Tehran. One Iranian told me about a local saying to the effect that half the telephones in Tehran could not dial out, but that was okay because the other half could not receive calls anyway.

* * *

Later on, I made my way down to the lobby to find something to eat. It was already afternoon and I hadn't even had breakfast. After getting off the elevator, I walked over to the table set up by our conference organizers. The man who had met us at the airport last night was sitting there by himself. He gave me a friendly greeting and then a mild scolding for not having gone on the bus tour with the others. "You will be here in Iran for only a short time. You can catch up on your sleep when you go home." I didn't think it would be prudent to tell this representative of officialdom that I had spent the past few hours making phone calls to my students' relatives.

I asked him to join me for lunch. Not being busy, he accepted. We went into the hotel's restaurant where we both started off with an "Islamic beer"--which, of course, was non-alcoholic. I wondered how it was that a teetotaller could make imitation beer without having tasted real beer. But after one sip, I concluded that the manufacturers of this Islamic beer must never have tasted the real thing since their product certainly didn't taste anything like it.

The "man from the desk" as I will call him (since I forgot his name) told me briefly about his career. Before the revolution, he had been the principal at a secondary school. One of his former students, Ali Akbar Velayati, was now the foreign minister. It was Dr. Velayati, the "man from the desk" acknowledged, who had arranged for him to work at the IPIS.

He outlined for me what our schedule would be in Iran. The next three days (Monday, Tuesday, and Wednesday) we would be preoccupied with the conference. But on Thursday and Friday, the Muslim weekend, we would be taken to the beautiful city of Isfahan. We would spend Saturday back in Tehran before flying out late that night.

It was generous of the institute to arrange for us to go to Isfahan, but this did not suit my own plans. I wanted to stay in Tehran so that I could meet as many of my students' relatives as possible. As lovely as Isfahan might be, I thought I would learn far more about current conditions in Iran from talking to as many people as possible away from the official program.

"I want to stay in Tehran over the weekend," I announced.

A look of annoyance crossed his face. "Why?" he demanded.

"I want to attend the Friday prayers at Tehran University." I had frequently read in the press that this event attracted a crowd of thousands each week and was often the venue of important speeches on the part of the Islamic leadership.

"I am not sure that will be possible," he responded.

"Oh, I hope it is," I said as politely as I could. "It is something I really want to see." We dropped the subject, but I feared that this man was going to try to thwart my plans--a fear which would prove to be well-founded.

* * *

That evening, the IPIS sponsored a dinner for the foreign and Iranian conference participants there at the hotel. What struck me immediately was that there were many Iranian women in the crowd. They were dressed conservatively with their heads covered, but their faces were entirely visible--unlike in most Arabian Peninsula countries where women's faces were either partially or completely hidden from view. These Iranian women were not at all shy about initiating conversations with men. Some even said openly that they did not agree with the dress code which they must conform to. I had thought that men and women would sit separately when dinner was served, but the Iranian women interspersed themselves among the men. They participated actively in conversations, laughing and joking frequently. And all this took place at what amounted to an official dinner. I had never seen women take part in and behave like this at an official dinner in the Arab world where strict segregation of the sexes was the norm in most countries.

At this dinner, I heard a theme in Iranian thinking that would be repeated frequently over the next three days. This conference was being held just weeks after the breakup of the USSR at the end of 1991. The Western press was already publishing stories about how Turkey and Iran were battling for influence in the newly independent republics of Central Asia. But while there was much speculation in the West over which country would win this contest, the Iranians had no doubt about its outcome: Iran would prevail. The Iranian conference participants all seemed to believe that Iranian culture and religion would be so attractive to the people of Central Asia that these republics would all gravitate toward Iran.

I pointed out that only the Tajiks in Central Asia spoke Farsi. All the others, including the Uzbeks who were the most populous group, spoke languages related to Turkish. An Iranian lady sitting across from me replied, "But Uzbeks *are* Persians."

The Iranians all recognized that Turkey had a linguistic link to Central Asia, but they insisted that Iran's cultural link was stronger. I asked them to tell me specifically what it was about Iranian culture which, even absent the linguistic link, would appeal so strongly to the Central Asians. The Iranians seemed to think that the answer was self-evident: not only was Persian culture appealing in its own right, but--to them anyway--was clearly superior to the culture of Turkey or any other nation which might compete with Iran for influence in Central Asia. While they saw the Islamic religion as also being a common bond between Iran and Central Asia, they seemed to think that admiration of Persian culture was a stronger one. This sense of the attractiveness of Persian culture to others is something that is shared by most Iranians--whether they are supporters or opponents of the Islamic republic.

* * *

The three days of the conference were exhausting. The sessions lasted from early morning until mid-evening each day. The conference was held at IPIS headquarters in North Tehran. The conference hall itself was quite large, and there were hundreds of people in attendance. Simultaneous translation between English and Farsi was provided by high quality interpreters.

The conference began on the first day with an opening prayer and then a speech by the foreign minister, Dr. Velayati. He discussed Iran's foreign policy initiatives vis-a-vis Central Asia and the Caucasus. He mentioned Iranian efforts to mediate the ongoing war between Armenia and Azerbaijan over Nagorno-Karabakh. I did not hear him utter any direct criticism of the United States or the West. The speech, I thought, was quite moderate.

The article about his speech that appeared the next day in *Tehran Times,* however, indicated that he had criticized the U.S. Velayati "warned against Washington's attempts to fill in the vacuum created in after [*sic*] the fall of communism," stated the article's first paragraph. "'Sources of instability in these republics can pave the way for the growing American influence in the region,'" he was quoted as having stated himself.[1]

And so I was initiated into the mysteries of trying to understand Iran. Had Velayati not said anything critical in his actual speech out of politeness since Americans were present in the audience? Or had the interpreter simply not translated this part of his speech into English? Which was the real message-- the more moderate one in the actual speech, or the more hard-line one in the newspaper? Or were the two messages intended for different audiences?

There were mixed messages about what kind of relationship Iran wanted with America throughout the conference. Several of the Iranian speakers called for improved Iranian-American relations. But each remark to this effect was usually followed by a harshly critical remark by another Iranian implying that improved relations were impossible. Some of these criticisms appeared to be made gratuitously. For example, one of the American participants had given a presentation designed to please (or, more accurately, pander to) the Iranian audience. Immediately afterward, the Iranian moderator for the panel said the following: "A Persian poet wrote about America long before it was even discovered. He said that there was a big country that made a big noise, but could do nothing else." The Iranians in the audience seemed to think that this remark was hilarious. But I couldn't understand his point: Why say something so critical of America after an American speaker had lauded Iran? What was the message they wanted us to take back to the U.S.? (The Iranians seemed to think that we were all quite highly connected in Washington--an impression that several of the Americans made unstinting efforts to further.) Had they gone to the expense of bringing us to Tehran simply to insult us?

Yet while there was a strong anti-American theme in the conference, also evident was an understanding that America was not the expansionist "Great Satan" they portrayed it to be. For example, the main point of my presentation was that despite the recent American interventions in Panama and Kuwait, the U.S. was less likely to pursue military intervention in the post-Cold War era because the American public and Congress were unlikely to see it as necessary in the absence of a global threat to American interests as the USSR had been. Not only was this viewpoint not challenged by the Iranians in the question-and-answer session (they were not shy about challenging me on other points), but in his speech at the end of the last day summarizing the "findings" of the conference, the head of the IPIS (who is also a deputy foreign minister) cited this very point.

What I concluded after listening to all their speeches was that the Iranian government itself was undecided about whether it was possible for Iran to have improved relations with the U.S. More importantly, though, I thought there were signs of a debate about whether the Islamic republic wanted to improve its ties to the U.S. even if this was possible. It struck me that some in the Iranian government found it useful to have America as an enemy in order to justify their undemocratic policies.

* * *

I was surprised to see so many women attending the conference. The Western women looked and felt awkward attempting to adhere to the rigid Islamic dress code. Some were wearing rain coats because none of the long skirts they brought were long enough by Iranian standards. Their scarves did not quite cover all their hair.

The Iranian women, of course, had long grown accustomed to the code. They all wore long black coats that covered even their ankles. Although their faces were uncovered, not one wisp of their hair was showing under their full black head scarves or *chodors*. Although women could now, after the death of Khomeini, reveal a little bit of hair above their foreheads in public, female government employees were still not allowed this freedom while at work. The site of a woman's hair, I was frequently told during the conference, might arouse men sexually, and this could not be risked inside government offices which were supposed to be upholding Islamic morality.

For the Western men, conforming to the Iranian male dress code was no problem: all we had to do was wear our suits but not our ties. We were right in style and felt comfortable too.

Just as at other conferences, some of the presentations were interesting while some were not. Also just as at other conferences, the most enjoyable parts of this one were not the formal sessions but the informal one-on-one conversations that took place during coffee breaks and lunches. People were often willing to reveal more of their thinking and personalities in a private conversation than in a public lecture.

During breaks for coffee and lunch on the first day, I observed what to me is always a fascinating process: how people who do not know one another initiate conversations and become acquainted. Iranian men and Western men did not hesitate to begin conversations with each other. Similarly, Iranian women and Western women were also able to talk to each other easily. I noticed, however, that Iranian men almost never initiated conversations with either Western or Iranian women. Indeed, they generally acted as if the women were invisible.

The Western women, though, refused to be ignored. They were not shy about introducing themselves to Iranian men and talking with them. By contrast, most of the Iranian women did not speak to any men. A few, however, did--and they were the ones who began these conversations.

I decided that I would not attempt to begin a conversation with any of the Iranian women for fear that doing so in a public setting would make them uncomfortable or get them in trouble. I realized (indeed, I hoped) that my concern might be overblown. The way to safely find out, I reasoned, was to wait and see if an Iranian woman initiated a conversation with me. But on the first day of the conference, I waited in vain.

* * *

My wait ended during lunch on the second day. Lunch each day was served in a buffet on two long tables on either side of a very large reception room. There were no chairs so we all had to eat standing up. I was with a group of four or five men. Two of them were arguing out a point raised in the previous session. I was not really paying attention and was looking around to see if there might be a more interesting group to join.

Off to my right, there were two young Iranian women talking together. When I first looked over at them, one of them was smiling and seemed to be looking directly at me. Not wanting to stare, I turned my attention back to the group I was with. But I soon looked back at the two women, and the same one was still looking at me and smiling even more broadly.

I nodded my head toward her. She nodded her head very slightly in return. I abruptly abandoned the group of men I was with and went over to join the ladies.

We introduced ourselves. The one who had been looking at me spoke English well; her name was Jabij. The other one, named Tourang, did not speak English quite as well. Both seemed happy to talk with me. They asked me about my life in America and I asked them about theirs in Iran.

The two women suddenly stopped talking and seemed quite nervous. I looked where they were looking. A young Iranian man was standing nearby, looking at me. "Excuse us," said one of the women. "He wants to talk to you," and they immediately moved away.

He did indeed want to talk to me, but I did not want to talk to him. He had made a particularly anti-American statement during one of the conference sessions that morning. But now he was obsequiously asking me if I would help him get admitted with a fellowship to study at my university.

I advised him that as a result of the Reagan administration's imperialist policy, which he had so eloquently described, all the money which had been available for foreign students in the past was now being used to fund increased covert CIA operations.

He shook his head and said he feared that this was the case. Just then, I spotted a colleague of mine from a Canadian university standing nearby. I suggested to the young man that since Canada was a peaceful country, it might have money for foreign students. I suggested that my Canadian friend would undoubtedly be extremely pleased to talk with him about this.

Without even saying good-bye, the young man went straight over to the Canadian professor (who later thanked me profusely for referring this young man to him and promised that he would do a similar favor for me one day). Just as the Iranian man left me, the two Iranian women came back.

I asked them, "Why did you go away when he came up to me? He could have waited for us to finish talking."

"Men do not wait for women here," said one. "We wait for them."

* * *

During the conference sessions, the Iranian women all sat together in the back of the room by themselves. I wanted to sit with Jabij and Tourang, but concluded that this would not be politically correct. I wondered whether I would be able to talk with them again.

During the afternoon coffee break, I noticed Jabij gliding toward me. As soon as our eyes met, she veered off and stood in an area where there were not too many people. I joined her. She complemented me on how quickly I was learning Iranian ways.

We talked about the conference sessions which we had just heard. Some of the Iranian speakers had again made simplistic statements about America, portraying the U.S. government as being controlled by Jews. I asked Jabij why the Iranian government bothered to bring us American professors to Tehran to listen to childish statements which the Iranian Foreign Ministry itself knew were nonsense.

She became defensive. She said that while she liked individual Americans, she did not like the U.S. government. In a bitter tone of voice, she said, "Your country has caused a lot of problems for mine!"

I told her that the feeling was mutual.

"But your country has caused far more problems for mine than mine has for yours," she asserted. Her face was flushed and angry. "One of the worst problems is that thanks to the American embargo, the economy here is in such bad shape that Iranian men have to go to the West--even to America--to find whatever jobs they can. Instead of staying here to build our country, they go to America to build yours!"

Conversations do not necessarily follow a logical course. Or, perhaps more accurately, they follow a logic of their own. In any event, I replied, "Maybe Iranian men aren't going to America and the West against their will. Maybe they prefer to be in a country where women don't have to dress the way you do."

This made her even angrier. "Iranian men may go to America, but they come back and marry Iranian women!"

I pointed out that not all Iranian women lived in Iran. "There are lots of Iranian women in America, and they dress and behave like American women."

Jabij seemed to undergo a complete transformation. Her mood changed from anger to wistfulness. "I know," she said softly. "They do everything. And that's good. For what each woman chooses is right for her."

Her voice became passionate: "What good is chastity if it is forced on a woman? If chastity has any value, it is only when a woman chooses it for herself when she is free to make other choices." Her face was radiant as she said this.

I told her I agreed with her. Laughing, she replied, "I thought you would."

As so many other Iranian women in Tehran did, Jabij asked me to describe how my female Iranian students dressed and behaved in America. She let out a cry of pleasure (and then looked around quickly to see if anyone had heard it) when I told her they often wore short skirts. All too soon, the conference started up again and we had to resume our seats.

* * *

At the end of each day at the conference, it took an hour or more for our bus to traverse Tehran's immense, tangled traffic jams. During the slow ride back after the second day, Tuesday, I was worried that the two gentlemen who were going to pick me up for dinner might grow impatient waiting and leave. But, I calculated, they were probably caught up in the same traffic jam that I was.

We finally made it back to the hotel. I walked slowly around the lobby. No one there seemed to be looking for me (we Americans did tend to stand out), so I went up to my room. The elevator, as usual, took a long time to arrive. After a large crowd got off, those of us waiting packed ourselves in. It stopped at nearly every floor. After what seemed like an interminable length of time at close quarters with a lot of strangers, the elevator finally reached my floor--the seventeenth. Within a couple of minutes of entering my room, the phone rang: it was the desk clerk saying that my friends had arrived and were waiting downstairs (it had been made clear to us that the elevator guards would only allow hotel patrons into the elevator, so there was no question of my guests coming up to see me). After putting down the phone, I went out for another long trip in the elevator down to the lobby.

When I finally got there, I looked around, but couldn't identify any pair of men who were waiting for me. I was just about to go over to the desk clerk and ask him if he could point out who had asked him to call me down when someone did approach me--a woman.

"Dr. Mark?" she enquired. It was hard to tell how old she was just from her face, but she seemed to be in her early twenties. After I owned up that I was indeed Dr. Mark, she introduced herself and asked me to come sit where her mother was in the coffee lounge in the middle of the lobby.

When the three of us were sitting down, the young woman explained that she and her mother were the cousin and aunt of one of my Iranian students. Their male relatives had been unable to come. We were just settling down to a pleasant conversation, when the institute's "man from the desk" rushed up and began speaking rather harshly in Farsi to the two women. They both stood up and began talking back to him. After a brief exchange, he stalked away, obviously annoyed.

The pleasant mood had definitely been spoiled. "What did he want?" I asked.

"He wanted to know why we were here talking to you and how we knew you," explained the daughter. " We just told him you were a friend of our relatives in America and that we were here to learn the news about our family from you."

The mother said something in Farsi. The daughter translated: "Does that man follow you everywhere?"

I said no, but they did not seem reassured. I wasn't either. Slowly, we managed to restore a pleasant atmosphere. When the coffee finally arrived, I insisted on filling their cups for them. This made them both laugh. No man had ever done such a thing for them before, the daughter told me.

Both of them questioned me in detail about how their cousin in America dressed. Like the other Iranian women on campus, I told them, she dressed stylishly--an observation that did not seem to surprise them. They were especially pleased to hear that she always wore her long hair out loose. Both mother and daughter shook their heads and smiled as they contemplated this.

At the end of the conversation, they told me that they could not have the dinner for me as planned tonight, but that the two male relatives would definitely come to pick me up on Thursday evening. As we got up and were saying good-bye, I noticed that the "man from the desk" was glaring at us. I realized that I would definitely have to miss the trip to Isfahan, which was scheduled to depart Thursday morning, if I was going to have dinner with these people.

* * *

The next morning before we boarded the bus, the "man from the desk" told me that he had made airline and hotel reservations for me for the trip to Isfahan. I told him I wanted to stay in Tehran. He feigned surprise and asked me why. I reminded him that I had already said I wanted to attend the Friday prayers at Tehran University. He again said he doubted this was possible. This time, however, he said that he would find out for me. I was fairly certain what the result of his inquiry would be.

How was I going to thwart this man? I wasn't sure I was going to be able to do so, but during the last day of the conference, an opportunity arose.

During one of the morning conference sessions, I found myself sitting next to an elderly cleric. He was coughing a lot, so I offered him one of the cough drops that I had brought with me. He didn't speak any English, but he conveyed his thanks to me in gestures. At the end of the session, he signaled that he would like to talk to me. The Iranian sitting on the other side of me volunteered to translate. In fact, I was a little surprised that a small crowd had gathered around us.

The elderly cleric asked me what I did in America, how I liked the conference, and how I liked Iran in general. He seemed very kind. I told him that the one thing I was really hoping to do while I was here was attend the Friday prayers at Tehran University. This ambition seemed to please him. I asked him if it would be possible. He responded that not only would it be possible, but he would see to it that I was taken there. He seemed to give directions to someone from the institute to this effect. He then said good-bye.

Several of the Iranians who had gathered around us remained. They told me that this man was a *hojatolislam*--the highest clerical rank in Shia Islam after ayatollah. They told me that he was particularly respected and loved because he was both kind and wise. They seemed very pleased that he and I had had a good conversation.

I suddenly realized that the image common in the West of Iranian clerics being filled with hate and venom was not universally accurate. An Iranian cleric could be kind and gentle, just as I had seen.

* * *

I saw Jabij during the coffee break after the first session on that third day of the conference, but she would not talk to me. I tried twice to catch her eye, but both times she turned and walked away from me. I thought that she had become embarrassed about revealing so much about her feelings during our last conversation and now she was avoiding me. I feared that she would not speak to me again.

But I was wrong. During lunch, I was talking with my Canadian colleague when he suddenly asked me, "Aren't you going to introduce me to your two lady friends?"

"I would if I knew where they were," I answered.

"But they're right behind you." And so they were. Jabij and Tourang seemed to be waiting for us to come talk with them.

During the previous session, one of the American participants made a particularly--indeed, panderingly--pro-Iranian statement. Even more, he had implied that his pro-Iranian viewpoint was widely held within the U.S. government. I informed the two women that he was speaking for himself alone.

Jabij said, "I'm glad you told me that because many of my colleagues think he was speaking on behalf of your government. Even now he is having a private lunch with one of our deputy foreign ministers." We all laughed. I was happy because now Jabij seemed comfortable talking with me again.

My Canadian friend and Tourang became engrossed in their own conversation, and so Jabij and I were left to talk with each other. "Individual Americans and Iranians can get along together," she said. "I wish something could be done to improve relations between our two countries."

Being a professor, I then launched into one of my pet lectures about how America was a nation of immigrants and how unlike other Western states with more homogenous populations, American policy toward other countries was often strongly influenced by the people living in America with ties to those countries. Groups which had good relations with the government of a country where they had ethnic ties, such as existed between American Jews and Israel, could influence Washington to support that government. But when ethnic groups in America had poor relations with the government of their "home country," such as existed between Cuban-Americans and the Castro regime, these groups could successfully lobby to prevent Washington from doing much to improve its relations with that government.

Therefore, I concluded, if Iran wanted to improve relations with the U.S. government, it must first improve its relations with the Iranians living in America. For if ties between the Islamic republic and Iranian-Americans remained poor, relations between Tehran and Washington were likely to remain poor too.

Jabij reacted angrily to my statement. "Why should we here have to court those rich Iranians who fled to America with our money. They've been over there for years living a hedonistic life while we've had to suffer!"

I told her that very few Iranian-Americans were rich. Most came with little money and have had a difficult time adjusting to life in America. Those who often had the hardest time were those who had been rich in Iran, came to America with no money, and had to take relatively menial jobs which barely supported them and their families.

"I don't believe it! They would say they're suffering if they had to do any work at all! All they know how to do is complain!" Jabij insisted. "They have no idea how we have suffered. We've had to live through years and years of war with Iraq. They don't know what it's like to be attacked by missiles! They don't know what it's like to stand in line for hours waiting to buy a small piece of bread!"

Her eyes narrowed and she asked, "Are those Iranian students of yours any good? The ones wearing the short skirts?"

I responded that they were not all the same. Like other students, some worked hard and some did not.

"I'll bet they're all worthless!" said Jabij. "I'll bet those girls spend more time in the beauty parlors than in class!"

Before I had a chance to reply, Jabij took Tourang by the arm and stalked off.

"I was having a perfectly nice conversation with Tourang," complained my Canadian friend. "I don't know what it was you said to Jabij, but I wish you had not said it."

* * *

I had brought some little presents with me from America--coffee mugs with my university's logo on them--to give to any friends I made. I had them with me now to give out at the end of the conference. During the afternoon session, I spotted Tourang and presented one to her.

She seemed genuinely delighted and thanked me profusely for thinking of her. I told her that I also wanted to give one to Jabij, but I could not find her.

Tourang offered to take me to her, but complained that Jabij and I spoke English so fast together that she could not keep up with us. Tourang urged me to "please speak slowly."

When we found Jabij, I offered her a mug. Unlike Tourang, though, she would not take it and became quite nervous. "I cannot be seen taking a present from you," she told me and moved away.

I thought of a remedy for the problem. I would ask one of the American women to give Jabij the mug for me. The first one I asked--Martha--agreed. As we were approaching Jabij, I gave the mug to Martha and stopped. Martha then walked up to where Jabij was sitting and gave it to her.

Jabij took the mug, jumped up from her seat, and practically shouted, "You didn't have to do that!"

"But you said you couldn't be seen taking it from me," I reminded her.

"Oh, I was just kidding then," said Jabij.

Martha gave me a bewildered look and walked away.

Jabij laughed, but then looked at me shyly. "Do you want to know why I am so anti-American?" she asked. She then told me about how she had been engaged to be married to an Iranian man who could not find a job in Iran. He went to the U.S. where he did find one. After awhile, he wrote and asked her to join him. Since the seizure of the American hostages, there has been no U.S. embassy in Tehran. Jabij flew to Switzerland in order to apply for an American visa. Her application was denied, so she went back to Tehran. Soon thereafter, her fiance broke off the engagement.

Now in her early twenties--Jabij would not tell me her exact age--she insisted that she was no longer marriageable. Looking truly miserable, she said, "And all because your government wouldn't give me a visa! There was no reason to deny me one--they just wanted to be cruel!"

She then rushed off. It was just as well since nothing I could have said would have comforted her.

* * *

An Iranian deputy foreign minister made the final speech which closed the conference. In his speech, he told something of a joke. During much of the conference, we had been debating whether Iran or Turkey--two longtime rivals--would be the country that successfully extended its influence to the newly independent Muslim republics of former Soviet Central Asia.

"You Westerners assume that this is an either/or question," he said. "But you forget that Islam allows for polygamy. Therefore, Central Asia can have Turkey and Iran, and it's okay!"

As I was leaving the conference hall, Jabij suddenly appeared at my side. She said that the minister had made a good point with his joke: Central Asia could have relations with both Turkey and Iran; it did not have to choose between them.

Like a typical professor, I had to argue with her. I told her that Central Asia might find it difficult to maintain good relations with Turkey and Iran at the same time, just as it must be difficult for a man with four wives to simultaneously keep them all happy.

She looked directly at me and smiled roguishly as she said, "*You* would enjoy polygamy." After she stopped laughing, she said more seriously, "Of course, you have to be able to support each wife and all the children."

"It would work better the other way around," I said. "Each of them could support me." I started to consider the ramifications more seriously: "If I had four wives and each earned fifty thousand dollars a year, I wouldn't have to work at all!"

"You're impossible!" she informed me.

Both of us became quiet. We each knew that the moment to say farewell had arrived. I told her that I had very much enjoyed talking with her and that I would think about some of the things she had said for a long time.

Suddenly, Jabij's anger flared up again: "Don't you tell those Iranian girls at your university anything I told you!"

But then just as quickly her anger died down. In a softer voice, she said, "I don't care what you tell them."

As we said good-bye, we could not exchange a kiss, a hug, or even a handshake. As I was repeatedly told while I was in Tehran, a handshake between an unrelated male and female was punishable by two days in prison for both. So Jabij and I each just walked away from each other.

But just as I was about to get on the bus which would return the foreign participants to our hotel, I turned around and looked back. There was Jabij looking at me and smiling, just as she had been the first time I saw her. She waved and then disappeared into a throng of other women dressed in black.

* * *

When I got back to the hotel that night, the "man from the desk" glared at me but said nothing. I presumed that he had been informed about my being given permission to stay in Tehran and go to the Friday prayer services. He seemed particularly annoyed when the father of one of my other Iranian students met me in the lobby to take me to dinner that evening. But this time, he did not say anything.

I was taken to an apartment somewhere in Tehran. It was beautifully decorated. Expensive Western and Iranian art work hung on the walls. My hostess was wearing a blouse and mini-skirt. Neither she nor the other lady present had her hair covered as is required in public.

Soon after arriving, I got into a debate with the Iranians. "You don't believe us!" exclaimed the hostess. "Were you taken in by the official propaganda?"

They had all been telling me that the Islamic regime was extremely unpopular. They insisted that the ruling clerics were both corrupt and incompetent. The women made it clear that they despised having to conform to the rigid dress code imposed by the mullahs.

"You're from the old elite," I responded. "It's not surprising that you oppose the Islamic regime. I just wonder if the ordinary citizens share your point of view."

"Okay," said my student's father. "I'm going to prove to you that the ordinary citizens oppose the regime too. Tomorrow I'm going to take you down to the Tehran bazaar."

The next morning, after the other Americans went off to Isfahan, my student's father came by in a taxi to take me to the bazaar. People there were surprised when he introduced me as an American. They immediately started complaining about the regime. Many said that the system of justice was utterly chaotic. One lawyer observed that clerics trained in fourteenth century theology simply didn't have the ability to make judgments about a modern, complex society.

In one shop, a young man begged, "Please do something for us!"

Many merchants wanted to know why the U.S. retained its economic embargo against Iran. "The ayatollahs can sell as much oil as they want to Western Europe and Japan. Your embargo only hurts people outside the government."

"Now do you believe me?" my student's father asked.

I shook my head. "These people are all merchants. They're not average citizens." (I later learned that the merchants of the Tehran bazaar were among the principle supporters of the Ayatollah Khomeini when he first came to power, so their complaining about the Islamic regime now was in fact an important change.)

"God, you are stubborn!" said my student's father. He frowned for a few seconds, but then smiled. "I know how I can prove to you that even ordinary citizens are fed up with this regime. Come on."

We got into a taxi. "Where are we going?" I asked.

"We're just going for a ride so I can prove my point," he answered.

* * *

In Tehran, people mill around intersections on the major thoroughfares, shouting out their destinations in the hope that a taxi, or even a private car, will give them a ride. There was an extraordinary number of people trying to get rides today, I was told, because the bus drivers were on strike.

To maximize their earnings, taxi drivers carry as many passengers as possible. Thus, our tiny little cab was crowded with as many as eight people during our two-hour ride.

People entering the cab instantly asked who the Westerner was. Upon being told I was American, they all had something to say. One man insisted on singing a song for me. Another told a dirty joke. Virtually everyone condemned the government. What especially amazed me was that they didn't seem to care if other Iranians they did not know heard them utter such sentiments. It was simply assumed that everyone present thought the same way.

One elderly lady got in the cab and was introduced to me. She practically shouted in English, "I hate the Islamic government!" She then said something in Farsi which made everyone else laugh uproariously. My friend translated: "She says that the mullahs are so corrupt that one of them demanded that she, an old lady, go to bed with him."

The cab ride became a moving seminar on the current ills of Iran. Among the many thoughts expressed were the following:

--Iran's current mess was all the fault of President Jimmy Carter who had advised the shah not to use force against his opponents. If only the shah could have kept the lid on until Ronald Reagan came to office, things would have been different.

--The shah was a pretty stupid guy; the fact that he listened to advice from Carter proved that. But life in Iran had been much better under him than under the mullahs.

--Iran possessed tremendous oil wealth, yet almost everyone was now poor and everything was getting shabbier. Where had all the money gone? Obviously, the clerics were pouring it into their Swiss bank accounts.

--The United States and Britain wanted the ayatollahs to rule Iran because they wanted Iran to be weak. It was obvious to Iranians that the Islamic regime couldn't last a day without Western support. I tried to disabuse them of this notion. Their expressions made it clear that they thought I was either a fool or a liar.

When the taxi finally dropped me off at my hotel, my student's father asked, "Now do you believe me?"

* * *

Later that afternoon, the brother of yet another one of my Iranian students came to the hotel to have coffee with me in the lobby. After we talked for awhile, we arranged that he would come pick me up Saturday morning to show me some sights in Tehran and then take me to his home for lunch. After he left, two Iranian ladies who were sitting nearby asked me to join them. They quickly began to complain about the status of women in Iran.

They said that coming to this hotel to have coffee and pastries in the lobby was the most exciting entertainment allowed to them under the present regime. One of them said bitterly, "We don't want to live like this. We're not Arabs--we're not fanatics!"

Most of the Persians I met expressed highly negative views about Arabs. "If the Arabs want to burden themselves with all this fundamentalist rigmarole, let them!" said the other lady. "We don't want it! We Persians are civilized! We're Europeans!"

"The Arabs are the cause of all our problems," said the first lady. "They imposed this crazy religion on us to begin with. We Iranians should go back to our own native religion--Zoroastrianism."

If the Iranian people didn't want this Islamic regime, I asked, then why was it still in power? "It is what America wants," said one lady. But the other one predicted that the regime "had to fall" within a year or two.

"Tell the American people," said one, "that Arab women may want to hide themselves away from men, but Persian women don't. Persian women are not shy."

The other one said that Persian women express their opposition to the law forcing them to cover their hair in public by leaving some of it exposed.

"Why did the mullahs impose such strict regulations on women?" I asked.

"They have some sort of complex about us," one of them shrugged.

* * *

I had been told that I would be picked up at eight o'clock that night by the relatives of the two ladies who had come to see me on Tuesday evening. I went to the lobby a little before that time. I ended up waiting until 9:30, but nobody came. I told myself at first that the delay was due to the terrible traffic, but finally I decided I had better call. When I phoned, the daughter whom I had met answered the phone. "Didn't you get our message?" she asked in surprise. There had been no message, I told her. "Oh," she said, "my grandmother suddenly became very ill. My mother and some of our other relatives are with her now. I'm so sorry."

I was too; I might have been able to make other plans if I had learned this earlier. I told her I was sad to hear about her grandmother, but somehow thought that this wasn't the real reason the dinner was canceled.

Before leaving Iran, I called again to enquire about how the grandmother was doing. If she really was ill, I thought I should tell her relatives back in America about it. The daughter answered the phone again. She sounded cold and distant. As soon as I began speaking, she hung up. Something was clearly wrong. I did not call back again.

Several months later, I found out what actually happened. The mother of my student paid a visit to Iran after I did. She told me that the two ladies I had met in the hotel lobby that Tuesday evening got into a taxi after they left me. A police car followed them all the way home. In addition, their telephone suddenly began malfunctioning more than usual--a problem that ended shortly after my departure. They had canceled the dinner out of fear of what the authorities might do if they saw me visiting their home. And they very much felt that they were being watched. It could only have been the "man from the desk" who had set in motion the harassment they received as a result of talking with me. I have no idea why he chose to harass these two and not my other visitors. Perhaps it was because these two were women.

* * *

I had been told that someone (from the IPIS, I presumed) would call on me Friday morning to take me to Tehran University. But no one ever did. Much as I didn't want to, I went down to the lobby to ask the "man from the desk" to help me. But there was no one at the desk--which was not really surprising since Friday is the Muslim holy day. And so I spent much of Friday looking out at a dramatic thunderstorm from my room until my student's father who had picked me up for dinner Wednesday and taken me for that long taxi ride yesterday came once again to take me out to dinner.

This time, he took me to the home of his sister, where he was staying. His sister's husband and daughter were also there. There were beautiful Persian rugs and antiques throughout the house.

Much of the conversation was similar to ones I had had earlier. It was much more pleasant, however, because we were sipping a very nice red wine produced by the underground economy.

I told them how at my conference we were discussing the future of former Soviet Central Asia. Iranian officials and scholars confidently predicted that the people of Central Asia would be so attracted to Iranian culture and religion that all these new republics would naturally gravitate towards Iran.

Everyone burst out laughing. "These clerics can't run their own country properly," said the aunt. "How do they expect to run anyone else's?"

We watched a video of Pavrotti visiting his native Naples. The Iranians were sad afterwards. "The Italians enjoy life," observed the brother. "Why can't we?"

The aunt asked a series of questions in a bitter tone of voice: "Why can't we have comedies on the TV? Why can't Iranian women sing in public? Why can't they let us have accurate news? When will we be able to live like normal people?"

She looked depressed. But then she smiled. "I don't want you to leave here feeling sorry for us," she said. "We Persians have a history of conquering our conquerors. Our culture is so strong and rich that we eventually absorb them.

"And this time," she added, "our conquerors are not foreigners, but come from our own people. So conquering them won't take all that long."

"Believe me," she said, "we will do it. You will see."

* * *

On Saturday morning, my other student's brother came to pick me up. He arrived with a friend; both men were artists. It was actually the friend's car that we drove in.

First we went to their shop downtown. They had art work for sale there, some of which was their own. Next we went to the carpet museum which had been built during the shah's era. The array of Persian carpets on display was nothing short of spectacular. After that, we drove across town to a museum featuring the paintings of a famous Persian miniaturist. The building itself was in poor condition, but the collection was magnificent.

We ended up at the home of my student's brother. It was practically a museum itself. The living room was filled with eighteenth and nineteenth century Persian art and antiques. Downstairs was a workroom where two employees were busy restoring antiques--another little business that my host ran.

As in other Persian homes I had visited, the women of the house wore Western clothes, went about with their hair uncovered, and did not keep themselves hidden because an unfamiliar man had come into their midst. But unlike other Persian households where the women and children began questioning me almost as soon as I entered, my friend's family seemed distinctly uninterested in talking to me. His wife, daughter, and son barely said hello and then largely ignored me. I was surprised because I doubted that having Western visitors to their home was all that common for them.

My host had invited his friend and me to stay for lunch. While we were waiting for it to be prepared, I inquired about the various antiques and paintings that were on display. On one side wall between the living room and the kitchen there was something which struck me as odd because it was not old and valuable like virtually everything else in the room. It was a rectangular box which was divided into dozens of little square slots. Iranian currency had been placed inside a few of the slots.

"What's this?" I asked.

"This is where we put contributions for the poor," my host responded.

On an impulse, I pulled out my wallet and stuck a thousand rial note (less than a dollar) into one of the slots.

Suddenly, the wife became very animated. "Thank you!" she cried. "That was really nice!"

Without any transition, she asked me, "Hey, would you like to see a video? It's about the Sufis." Sufism, a Muslim religious sect, was a subject I knew almost nothing about.

When I assented, the wife became even more animated. Her son and daughter also expressed enthusiasm as we all sat down to watch. My host's friend, though, looked distinctly uneasy.

As soon as the film began, it was obvious that this was not a commercial production, but a home-made one instead. The opening scene showed about a dozen men dancing or whirling in a religious fervor. People in the crowd around them were chanting and shouting encouragement.

A man who appeared to be the leader of the group paced rapidly back and forth in front of the dancers. He held a curved sword upright in front of him. Suddenly he stopped, grasped the sword in both hands, and thrust it horizontally into his mouth--blade first.

This action was repeated several times. Behind him, the dancers were working themselves up into an increasing frenzy. One young man, who seemed to be in a particularly excited state, stepped toward the leader and rolled up his left sleeve. The leader handed his sword to someone else. He then took a dagger and thrust it through the young man's lower inner arm. The young man appeared quite pleased with this state of affairs.

I, on the other hand, was not. Everyone else, though, acted as if this was quite normal. The wife in particular was enjoying the video.

An even better scene came next. Another young man stepped forward with a frighteningly ecstatic expression on his face. With his left hand, he reached inside his mouth and pulled his left cheek outward. The leader then plunged a dagger through the cheek. The young man continued to pull at his mouth. The leader then inserted another dagger (he seemed to have an inexhaustible supply) inside the young man's mouth. The film showed the blade of the dagger piercing outward through the same cheek as before.

Most of the people watching cheered at this. But I was not feeling cheerful at all. Although hungry when I arrived at the house, by now my appetite for lunch had completely disappeared.

Mercifully, the scene shifted away from Mr. Dagger Mouth. The camera now focused on a group of people, including women as well as men, who were eating something from a common bowl. They too were in an ecstatic frenzy.

"What are they eating?" I asked timidly.

"Ground glass!" the wife answered enthusiastically.

I could not prevent myself from groaning.

The son and daughter both looked at me and laughed. "I eat it too!" said the boy. "It's good!"

"We do it for Allah!" added the wife with her usual zeal.

I suddenly realized that this video was something more than just a curious documentary that the family had somehow acquired. My suspicions were confirmed by the next scene which focused on the group of dancing men. After a few seconds, I recognized that one of them was my host!

I involuntarily let out a cry of horror and shuddered violently. One of my contact lenses fell out. "I've lost a lens!" I shouted.

Someone turned off the video. With concerned expressions, the family all gathered around me. I doubted that they knew what a contact lens was, and so grew afraid that they might crush it.

"Is that it?" asked the father doubtfully, pointing toward the carpet. It was. Fearing one of them might mistake it for an hors d'oeuvre, I snatched the lens up quickly.

I thrust it into my eye and a sharp pain immediately ensued; the carpet had obviously been dusty. As unpleasant as this was, however, I was grateful for the sensation since it allowed me to focus on something other than the growing nausea in my stomach.

I then stood up and announced, "I have to leave immediately! I have an appointment at the hotel!" Everyone knew I was lying, but I didn't care. I just wanted to get out of there.

"I'll drive you back!" my host's friend volunteered. It was clear that he was as eager to leave as I was.

After a perfunctory good-bye, my savior and I got in his car and took off. We were both sweating.

Neither of us spoke at first. He finally broke the silence. "My friend is a great artist, and I respect him very much. But I can't understand why he eats glass or lets himself be stabbed."

My sentiments exactly!

* * *

Just after being dropped off at the hotel, I met one of the other conference participants in the lobby. He told me that the trip to Isfahan had been wonderful. They had gotten back last night, and this morning there had been an informal meeting for the conference participants at the IPIS. He told me that some of us had been invited to go to the Foreign Ministry that afternoon while others had been invited to visit Tehran University. We had all been invited to a special dinner before our plane departed late that night. "Do you know where you are supposed to go?" he asked me. Since I did not, he suggested that I ask the "man from the desk," who had been staring at us as we spoke.

When I asked him whether I had been invited to either the ministry or the university, he responded stiffly, "You have not been invited to anything."

He then asked me whether I had liked my visit to the prayer services at Tehran University yesterday. I replied that I had not gone; I had thought someone from the institute was going to take me, but no one showed up.

"I'm so sorry," he remarked insincerely, "but I thought you had already arranged everything."

Clearly, I was being punished for not having gone to Isfahan with the rest of the group and for all my private, non-official meetings. I wondered, though, whether the decision to snub me like this had been made by the IPIS leadership or by the "man from the desk" all by himself.

* * *

While all my colleagues were visiting either the Foreign Ministry or the university, and later attending the special farewell dinner, I remained alone in my hotel room. Late that night, we all got back in the bus one last time for the trip to the airport. Instead of the VIP treatment he had given us when we first arrived in Tehran, the "man from the desk" pointed to where we were supposed to go, waved good-bye, and left. This time, our bags--along with everyone else's--were very carefully searched. After a long process, we all converged at the gate for our flight. In due course, we got on board the Air France jet whereupon the women in our group removed the scarves and raincoats they had been wearing for the past week. Shortly after take-off, the Air France stewardesses started serving alcohol. We had definitely left Iran.

Note

1."Iran Sensitive towards Central Asia," *Tehran Times*, March 3, 1992, pp. 1, 15.

Moroccan Dialogue

The call came on a Wednesday in June 1994. "Can you fly to Morocco this Saturday for a conference?"

It was a friend of mine at the International Republican Institute (IRI)--one of the relatively new organizations in Washington devoted to assisting the spread of democratization. The IRI is affiliated with the Republican party, but not actually part of it.

Someone on the original IRI delegation had dropped out at the last minute from the upcoming conference on "Local Government and Popular Participation" being held in Rabat. I was being asked to give two ten minute talks: one on the importance of transparency in government and the other on the role of the media as a link between citizens and government.

I said that these were not subjects that I knew much about. They were not to be authoritative lectures, I was told, but simply talks to stimulate a dialogue with the audience on these themes.

They didn't have to twist my arm much. I'd never been to Morocco before and definitely wanted to see it. I doubted I could make much of a contribution to Morocco's democratization, but if nothing else I hoped to get some more material for this book.

* * *

On the flights from Washington to Paris and Paris to Rabat, I read through part of the thick IRI briefing book on Morocco. The country had a parliament, but some of the articles in the briefing book indicated that the election process was manipulated by the government, and hence was the focus of opposition criticism. Still, opposition parties and opposition newspapers were allowed to exist--something unusual in the Arab world.

Nevertheless, the prime minister was not chosen by the parliament, but was appointed by the king--to whom he and the cabinet were responsible.

On the local level, there were elected mayors and councils. But the Moroccan equivalent of state governors were not elected; they were appointed by the king. This was similar to the system of local government existing in France (Morocco's former colonial ruler) until relatively recently. But in France, of course, the prefecture chiefs had been appointed by an elected official--the president. Such was not the case in Morocco.

Morocco, then, was a complex country. It was clearly not a full-fledged democracy, but it possessed certain elements of democracy--far more than any other Arab country I had visited. But where exactly did the balance between authoritarianism and democracy lie? And in what direction was the kingdom headed? I hoped our short visit might give me some insight.

* * *

When my plane touched down in Rabat, there was an honor guard and military band waiting. Much to our disappointment, these were not meant for the IRI delegation, but for President Nelson Mandela of South Africa, who had stopped in Morocco on his way to the Organization of African Unity summit in Tunis.

From the airport, we were taken to La Tour Hassan--famous as one of Rabat's grand old hotels. I thought the rooms were a little shabby, but the place certainly had atmosphere. The ornate hotel bar (unlike most Middle Eastern countries, alcohol is openly available in Morocco) seemed like the set for a movie. This was where the full delegation met up for the first time that evening.

After a few drinks there, our group moved over to the hotel's elegantly decorated Moroccan restaurant where we consumed an extraordinarily delicious feast. The delegation consisted of a former U.S. senator, two former U.S. ambassadors, one former mayor, two professors, and two IRI staffers. We decided to talk about what we were going to do at our two-day conference which would begin tomorrow morning.

We all acknowledged the importance of not lecturing to the Moroccans, but of "getting a dialogue going." We tried to think how best to do this. Someone suggested that the American speakers directly pose questions to the Moroccan audience to start the dialogue. Someone else proposed that we let the Moroccan participants speak first. This would show that we were not arrogant Americans trying to impose our views on the Moroccans, and would give the American speakers the chance to respond to what the

Moroccans had said--thereby initiating the (yes, by now you know) dialogue. Yet another person suggested that if the speakers' chairs were raised on a platform, the Americans immediately move them down into the audience in order to promote... Others in the group, though, felt that this might be just a little too insurgent--something Democrats would do, but not Republicans.

There appeared to be only one or two small flies in all this ointment of anticipated dialogue. The senior IRI staffer told us that apart from the keynote speaker, we still had not been informed as to who the Moroccan participants in the conference would be or what they would talk about. And the keynote speaker was to be the minister of the interior and information-- the individual in charge of the security services which were periodically employed to crack down on opposition parties and papers. Those most familiar with the country voiced the suspicion that the Moroccan organization which was co-sponsoring our conference, the Center for Strategic and International Studies at Mohammed V University, had close links with this particular ministry.

After such a wonderful meal and conversation, however, these did not appear to be very important problems. It was our conference, after all, and we would be managing it.

* * *

The next morning, we were picked up at the hotel and driven to the university. We were pleased to see that there were small announcements at the entrance of the university advertising our conference. The conference hall itself was similar to large university lecture halls everywhere: the speakers' table was indeed raised on a dais, and the seats for the audience were fixed to the floor in tiers rising upward with each successive row. There was no question of rearranging the furniture to promote dialogue.

We now received--when it was too late to change it--the Moroccan version of the conference program. After the opening address by the minister of the interior and information, there would be four sessions: one in the morning and one in the afternoon of each of the two days of the conference. The first three sessions would each consist of three Moroccan speakers as well as three American ones. The final session would consist of four Moroccans and four Americans.

The American delegation rapidly caucused. We would have to keep our remarks very short indeed to ensure that there was plenty of time for dialogue with the audience at the end of each session.

There were approximately 150 people in the audience. Not only were there students and professors, we were told, but several members of parliament as well as journalists. Word came that the minister would be delayed. We decided to start the conference so as not to keep the audience waiting. After an impromptu opening (in which the former senator unfortunately referred to Morocco as Mexico), the first session began.

The Moroccan participants readily accepted our proposal that they speak first. Despite being told that each speaker would be limited to only ten minutes, each of the Moroccans proceeded to read out loud (not simply speak from notes) mind-numbingly dull papers filled with all sorts of statistics and description. The papers in this session were more on economic development issues than politics.

The third of these presentations was happily interrupted by the arrival of the minister, Driss Basri. In his speech, Basri noted that local government has traditionally been strong in Morocco, and that this trend has continued since independence. He quoted King Hassan II as stating in 1989, "We will make of decentralization the best rampart against dictatorship," and in 1986, "We always thought that local councils are the authentic school of democracy." The minister even claimed that reforms introduced in 1976 which expanded decentralization and the role of municipal councils have "led the world to consider the Moroccan experience as a model."

Democracy at the local level was obviously alive and well in Morocco, at least according to the minister. Because his speech was filmed, the room was floodlit while he was talking. The audience burst into applause when he finished. Taking no questions, he left immediately. About half the audience left with him. When the interrupted morning session resumed, the room seemed especially forlorn in normal light and half empty.

* * *

When their turn to speak finally came, the three Americans each gave short little presentations so that we could finally get to the dialogue. But after the third American gave his talk, the Moroccan chairman of the panel declared that we would now break for lunch. The question-and-answer period for the morning session would be held before the afternoon session began. But after we got back from lunch, we launched straight into the afternoon session without having any dialogue with the audience about the morning session.

I was one of the speakers for the afternoon session. By now, there were only about fifty people in the audience. The room was sweltering. It was all I could do to keep awake while the three Moroccans on this panel also read through long, tedious papers. These, at least, seemed to have something to do with local government. But they mainly appeared to be statistical compilations on tax revenues received by local authorities, numbers of people elected to office at the local level, and other factoids.

When it was our turn to speak, the three Americans on the dais each gave short little talks. The time for dialogue had finally arrived. It was the former senator who chaired this panel. He asked for questions from the audience. One hand was raised by a Moroccan professor sitting in the front row. When he was duly called upon, he proceeded to read out loud (apparently the favored method of intellectual discourse in Morocco) a long, three-part question relating to the details of Moroccan local government which he addressed to the Moroccan panelists. This was discussed at some length. Afterward, the senator asked for additional questions. None were forthcoming, and so the afternoon session came to an end.

* * *

That night, the American participants ate dinner at a restaurant near the hotel. We all complained about what had happened the first day and talked about how we would change things tomorrow. But we all basically knew it was hopeless.

And indeed, the second day of the conference was very similar to the first day. In the morning, the Moroccans made long presentations, the Americans made short ones, and it was again declared that there was not enough time for any discussion before lunch, but that the question-and-answer period for the morning would occur immediately after it. Again, however, we did not hold a Q&A period after lunch but launched immediately into the afternoon session. Only when these speeches ended did the discussion period finally arrive. But the only hand to be raised was that of the same Moroccan professor who had posed a question yesterday. He again read out a long, three-part question which was addressed to the Moroccan speakers. When that was finally dispensed with, a closing ceremony was held in which the results of the conference were floridly praised. Then it was over.

The second day of the conference, though, was better than the first day in certain respects. In the morning session, one of the Moroccans who read a paper actually talked about opposition points of view. He noted in particular how the opposition parties wanted elected local governments to be more powerful than the central government was willing to allow. Indeed, it was possible to interpret his entire presentation as a veiled criticism of Moroccan government policy.

The other improvement on this second day was that even though there was no real public dialogue during the conference, I was able (as were others in the American delegation) to have several private dialogues in which individual Moroccans expressed a variety of viewpoints.

A Moroccan professor I met during the break in the morning session was especially frank. "This conference," he told me just after we had been introduced, "is a complete farce! It was arranged by the Moroccan and the American governments as propaganda so that Americans will think there really is democracy here!" He seemed especially incensed that he had learned about the conference only a few days in advance.

He was wearing what I thought of as the uniform of a North African leftist intellectual trying to imitate a French leftist intellectual. He had on an orange shirt, purple jacket, brown pants, and no tie. His forehead seemed to be arched in a perpetual pose of irony which he was probably now incapable of relaxing.

I told him that we Americans had virtually no control over the conference and had only learned who the Moroccan speakers would be at the start of it. This he would not accept. As with so many other Arab leftists I have known, he insisted that his own government could not possibly have done this on its own; the Americans "had to have been behind it."

We argued on inconclusively. He expressed great contempt both for what the Moroccan government called and what the American government seemed to accept as democracy in his country. I noticed later, however, that his contempt was not so great that he would refuse the Interior Ministry's invitation to lunch at a fancy beach hotel for the conference participants.

* * *

At that lunch, I sat next to someone who on the first day of the conference had been one of the government's strongest defenders. Much to my surprise, this gentleman today told me that he was in fact a critic of the government, especially on the issue of human rights. Just before our conference, he told me, he had attended a conference on human rights in Morocco. There, he said, he had given a speech which was "very hard" against the government.

"You must understand about Morocco," he told me, "that you can say or publish whatever you want. There are only three things that cannot be challenged: 1) the fact that Islam is the religion of Morocco; 2) the fact that Morocco is a monarchy; and 3) the policy toward Western Sahara." Western Sahara is the former Spanish colony just south of Morocco which the dictator Franco gave to Morocco shortly before his death. Since then, the Moroccan government has fought a sporadic war against an Algerian-backed guerilla group, POLISARIO, which has sought independence for the region.

"But these are three things that no Moroccan would challenge anyway," my lunch partner informed me. The two other Moroccans at the table nodded in agreement.

If his speech at the human rights conference had really been so critical of the government, I wanted to ask my lunch partner, why had his speech at our conference been so uncritical? I had the feeling that if his previous speech had been as hard as he said it was, he would not have been participating in our conference at all.

* * *

During the afternoon coffee break that day, I struck up a conversation with a young woman who was a journalist. Like so many other Western-dressed Moroccan women present, she was wearing jeans and a blouse. Her long black hair was uncovered. And she was fond of laughing.

Instead of the conference, our conversation focused on a comparison of our two careers. While there were many differences, we concluded that there were two ways in which they were similar. On the positive side, journalists and professors were able to avoid being stuck in an office all day. Both careers allowed for more freedom of movement than other occupations. On the negative side, neither journalists nor professors were paid very generously--though I suspect her complaints on this score were far more justified than mine.

I mentioned to her that it would be impossible for she and I to talk together openly like this in most other Arab countries. She readily agreed. "Morocco is a civilized country," she explained.

When the time drew near for the conference to start up again, I told her that I had enjoyed meeting her and, as I usually do with new acquaintances at conferences, gave her my business card.

Holding the card in her hand, she looked at me mischievously and asked, "Why are you giving this to me?"

I became embarrassed. "If you don't want it, I can take it back."

"No, no!" she responded. "It's mine now. Just answer the question."

"Well, if you ever come to Washington," I said, "you could call me up."

She laughed at this. "I don't think my boss would ever pay the money to send me to Washington! But if he does, I will call you," she said as she put the card in her purse.

"And do you have a card?" I asked.

"Of course not. Journalists don't carry them here. And why would I need one? I call people to interview them. They don't call me."

"But what if I had an exclusive story? Wouldn't you want me to call you instead of another journalist so that you could be the one to break the news?"

"You mean, `the scoop?'" she asked, laughing at the word.

"Exactly."

Suddenly she became very serious. "Do you have a scoop? If you do, you must give it to me immediately!" she practically shouted.

I told her that I didn't have any scoops.

Now she seemed crestfallen. "You don't have a scoop?" she asked in utter dejection.

I apologized for not having one.

Brightening up again, she said, "Well, if you don't have a scoop, then you don't need to call me. And if you don't need to call me, then you don't need my card!" She laughed triumphantly at this.

I had to admit there was a certain amount of logic in what she had said.

"Actually," she explained, "the reason why the journalists in my office don't carry business cards is because our boss does not want to spend the money to buy them."

I pointed out that she herself could pay to have some made up. The look of astonishment on her face told me that this was not an idea that had ever occurred to her before, and it was clearly not one she was going to adopt.

The conference was just about to start. I realized that I did not even know her name, and so I asked her what it was.

"I think it might be too difficult for you."

"Oh come on; what is it?"

She shrugged her shoulders, and then said her name. She was right. I could not catch it. It seemed to have five syllables. I asked her to repeat it.

She laughed and said, "I told you so! It's a Berber name, not an Arab one." The Berbers settled in North Africa long before the Arab conquest.

She said her name again, but all I could make out was that it began with an "M."

I shook my head in defeat. "Now I see there is another reason why you should get business cards--so that the people you interview can study your name and have a better chance of pronouncing it."

Her face lit up. "I will tell that to my boss! Maybe then he'll buy cards for me!"

We said good-bye and dashed to our respective seats.

* * *

After the closing ceremony and just before all the Americans were taken back to the hotel, I fell into conversation with Aminah--a young, vivacious Moroccan woman who was a graduate student at the university where our conference was held. She was wearing jeans, a blouse, and a suit jacket. Her long black hair flowed freely down her head and across her shoulders.

As we were talking, two women dressed in traditional Muslim garb with their hair covered in white scarves walked past us.

I asked Aminah what she thought of her "sisters."

She rolled her eyes and said, "Not for me!"

"Aren't you worried about the possibility of Islamic revolution?"

"It will never happen here in Morocco," she predicted confidently.

"But it is happening right next door in Algeria. Why couldn't it spread here?"

She laughed at this. "You Americans think we Arabs are all alike. But we're not. The most basic thing you must understand about Moroccans and Algerians is that we hate each other.

"We do not want Islamic revolution here anyway," she continued. "But if the Algerians have one, then we definitely don't want one because we would never want to be like them!"

* * *

Later that evening after it was all over, four of us American delegates who did not have other plans met in the hotel lobby before going to dinner. There was a Moroccan gentleman there who one of us recognized as having remained in the diminished audience for our conference. He introduced himself as a former member of parliament and asked if he could join us. We readily agreed.

At dinner, it became clear that he was quite a nationalist as well as an enthusiastic supporter of the king. We asked him, as someone with inside information about how Moroccan politics really worked, to tell us the extent to which the country actually was a democracy. We told him that we were confused; in some ways it seemed quite democratic, but in others not at all.

By this time, we had all partaken liberally of Morocco's excellent wine or beer. A warm spirit of camaraderie had developed.

"I will tell you honestly," said our Moroccan friend, "there is no democracy here at all. There is one-man rule."

He likened the rule of King Hassan II to that of Franco in Spain. But far from deploring this state of affairs, our friend saw it as highly praiseworthy.

"Like Franco, our king understands that the attempt to foster democracy in a country with insufficient economic and educational development will lead to chaos. Only when the economy has been developed and the populace educated can people be entrusted to handle democracy maturely and not fall for the false promises of revolutionary groups."

* * *

I felt that I had finally had an open dialogue with a Moroccan. Although I did not agree with him, I had to admit that our friend's argument contained a certain degree of logic. King Hassan II probably presides over the most liberal and civilized regime in the Arab world. Compared to the chaos and turmoil that other Arab countries appear to be falling victim to, it is no wonder that America and the West support him so strongly.

Still, there were some troubling questions about what I was sure was not just our friend's, but the Moroccan leadership's logic. Who will determine when the Moroccan people are economically and educationally prepared for democracy--the people or the king? Will an increasingly educated population be patient with the king's gradual approach to democratization, or at some point will it demand more rapid progress? In the latter case, would the king actually surrender power to elected institutions, or would he try to forcefully suppress popular demands for political change? And if he does this, will Morocco succumb to the mounting political and religious violence that other Arab states are experiencing?

Unfortunately, these are not questions that can be openly discussed in Morocco. Dialogue there definitely has its limits.

A Dip in the Gulf

The phone doesn't usually ring at 7:15 a.m. But it did that morning in late May 1994. It turned out to be someone from a new research institute in Abu Dhabi, capital of the United Arab Emirates (UAE). The institute was called the Emirates Center for Strategic Studies and Research. It was organizing a two-day conference on the latest civil war in Yemen which had recently broken out. The conference would be held in Abu Dhabi at the end of July-- less than two months away. Five Western scholars, including myself, were being invited to deliver papers on various aspects of the conflict. Was I interested in attending?

I certainly was. The problem with studying Yemen, I had discovered, was that no one besides others who studied Yemen cared much about what happened there. Opportunities for a sustained discussion of Yemeni affairs being rare, I was eager to attend this conference and hear what other scholars had to say. In addition, the UAE was a country on the Arabian Peninsula I had never been to, and so I wanted to see what it was like. And since the center was flying us all over in business class and putting us up at a five-star hotel, this promised to be more enjoyable than the typical academic conference which provided economy class tickets and mediocre hotel accommodations at best.

* * *

During the two-month Yemeni civil war, Saudi Arabia, Kuwait, and the UAE had all backed the South's effort to secede from the rest of Yemen. They were still furious with the government in the North for being supportive of Saddam Hussein during the 1990-91 Gulf War. The Saudis also had a territorial dispute with the Yemenis; they may have calculated that there was a better chance of settling this in their favor if there were two Yemens instead of one. But despite Saudi, Kuwaiti, and UAE support for the South, the North completely defeated its attempt to secede about two weeks prior to the conference.

Relations between the victorious North on the one hand and the states which had supported the South on the other had become extremely poor. Somehow or other, the Yemeni government had found out about the upcoming conference in Abu Dhabi. I got a phone call from a Yemeni cabinet minister warning me that Dr. Jamal Al-Suwaidi, the center director in Abu Dhabi, was rabidly anti-Yemeni. The Yemeni minister expressed the fear that the UAE government was somehow going to use the Western participants to add credibility to its "anti-Yemeni propaganda."

I assured him that as far as I and the other Western participants were concerned, this was simply an academic conference we were attending. But I too was a little worried. The UAE government had in fact supported the South during the war. Would the UAE participants use the conference simply as a platform to condemn the North?

* * *

Upon arriving in Abu Dhabi, each of the five speakers was met at the airport even before passport control. From there on, we were treated like VIPs: we were whisked through immigration and customs to a waiting Mercedes. But even the very short period of time spent outside before getting into the car was shocking. It was both the hottest and the most humid weather I had ever experienced. And this was late at night. Tomorrow I would learn how much more atrocious the weather was during the day. Going from an air conditioned car or building outside would lead to sunglasses steaming up instantly.

The next day was a rest day after our long flights; the conference would start the day after. In the morning, three of us were taken on a car tour of Abu Dhabi. This was definitely a modern city, for there was virtually nothing old in it. Almost all the buildings we saw were modern, though they could be divided into old new buildings (dating from the 1960s and 1970s) and new new buildings (everything more recent). The only historic building we saw was the old amiri palace downtown, and even that did not look particularly old. In parts of the city, especially on the way to the new amiri palace, lush vegetation lined the streets--an extraordinary feat in this desert land which must have been accomplished at an extraordinary cost.

Only about twenty percent of the UAE's population, we were told, are actually citizens of the country. The rest are foreigners who come to work in the UAE where jobs are more abundant or higher paying (or both) than in their own countries. As on previous trips to the region, I saw in the UAE people from many countries--especially South and Southeast Asia--working there. But on this trip I saw a group which I had never before seen in this part of the world: Russians. In our hotel alone, I met Russian women working at the reception desk, coffee shop, and bar. There was also a Russian man there, but I never figured out what he did. Someone told me that Russians were now working all over the UAE. On an afternoon trip to Dubai after the conference, we walked past a store with a sign which read, "Store for Russians," in Russian.

The Russians seemed awkward and out of place here. Since there had been no concern for making a profit back in the old USSR, the people working behind Soviet counters did not exactly worry about pleasing their customers. Here, however, the need to do just this was something that they had to learn quickly, as they would lose their jobs and be deported if they offended the wrong person in the UAE.

* * *

That afternoon, the four Western scholars who had already arrived were brought to the center to meet its director, Dr. Al-Suwaidi. He had earned his Ph.D. in political science from the University of Wisconsin at Milwaukee. We soon discovered that he was fluent in English, highly intelligent, and very personable. We had a lively discussion with him which whetted our appetites for the conference to begin.

Jamal then took us on a tour of the center. Everything about it was superlative. The conference room was elegantly appointed with a long table and comfortable chairs around it. It was also equipped with all kinds of electronic gadgetry to accommodate virtually any kind of presentation. In other parts of the center, there was machinery linking it with every important data base in the world. The amount of information it received was staggering. We who worked at underfunded universities in the West were envious.

There were a number of scholars both from the UAE and other countries working there. The UAE scholars tended to be younger. Jamal made it clear that he regarded part of his mission as molding UAE students who had done well at university into professional research analysts. As far as he was concerned, the UAE had relied too much on foreigners for this in the past.

We were introduced to several of the analysts at the center, including one young woman who followed Yemen. I had already noticed that while foreign women were relatively free to wear what they pleased, local women all wore the traditional long black robe and kept their heads covered. Outside, they usually wore veils covering the lower part of their face. Inside an office, though, they didn't veil, and could obviously work alongside men--unlike in neighboring Saudi Arabia.

When introducing us to this particular woman, Jamal told us that a few months before the 1994 Yemeni civil war broke out she had written a study predicting that it would occur and how it would end.

"I said that the North would win," she said.

One of our group asked why it was that the UAE government had been supportive of the South during the conflict.

"No one listens to us scholars!" Jamal explained. This was something I had frequently heard American scholars say.

* * *

The conference met over the next day and a half. There were five sessions during which each of the Westerners would present a paper. A general discussion would follow. Although the audience was entirely from the UAE, it was a diverse group consisting of diplomats, soldiers, professors, and even a short story writer. All seemed relatively young, though it was rather hard to tell with their heads and the sides of their faces covered in the headdress worn by men in this part of the world.

The discussions were very lively. The UAE participants freely challenged us as well as each other. They did not directly criticize their government for having supported the South, but many of them indicated that this had not been the most productive policy. They openly expressed their dislike for many aspects of Saudi policy. For the Saudis were not only pressing territorial claims against Yemen, but against the UAE and virtually every other country on the Arabian Peninsula. Others--especially the short story writer--expressed dismay over the chronically violent nature of Yemeni politics. Toward the end of the conference, several of the UAE participants indicated that instead of a weak, divided Yemen, the UAE was better off with a strong united one. While Saudi Arabia could always play two Yemens off against each other, the smaller states of the Arabian Peninsula (such as the UAE) could more easily work with a united Yemen to keep the Saudis in check.

* * *

Never had I attended a conference in the Arab world where there had been such an open expression of ideas as well as a complete lack of ideological dogma. Indeed, it was one of the best conferences I had ever participated in anywhere.

Why was Jamal's center so different from other research institutes and universities in the Muslim Middle East? Why was his so open while others were not? I would like to think that it had something to do with Jamal and so many of his staff having been educated in the United States, but this is not a distinction unique to them. There are plenty of professors and scholars in the Muslim Middle East who were educated in the West, but this seems to have done little or nothing to increase the openness of their institutions--or even their own minds in all too many cases. It is true that Jamal's center has very high level connections within the UAE which have allowed it to operate independently. But the heads of centers and universities elsewhere in the Arab world also have high level connections which do not want such organizations to operate freely.

What, then, is the explanation? Part of it has to do with Jamal himself. He possesses a genuine intellectual curiosity, a passionate commitment to rigorous research, and an appreciation for how debate can lead to greater understanding of an issue. But as laudable as they are, such attributes are surely not unique to Jamal in all the Muslim Middle East. What perhaps is unique is that such a person would be permitted--even encouraged--to run a research center in this part of the world. The fact that Jamal is doing so, then, says something not just about him, but about the UAE. While the UAE may not be a democracy, it does appear to be more tolerant than other countries in the region.

* * *

The day after the conference ended, I took an early morning flight from Abu Dhabi to Doha, capital of nearby Qatar. I had been invited to pay a visit there by the Qatari ambassador in Washington who had heard that I would be attending the conference in Abu Dhabi.

As soon as the plane door opened and before anyone could descend the stairs, someone entered the aircraft and called out my name. While everyone else piled into an airport bus, I was ushered into the back seat of a Mercedes and rushed to the VIP lounge. Someone took my passport to get it stamped while I was being served tea. I was then escorted to another Mercedes and taken to the Foreign Ministry.

I soon found myself in the large office of someone who was both a senior official and a young man simultaneously. He was fluent in English and very bright. We also talked about the recently ended Yemeni civil war. I asked why it was that while Saudi Arabia and the other Gulf Cooperation Council (GCC) members had backed the failed attempt by the South to secede and re-establish an independent state, Qatar alone had openly expressed support for the maintenance of Yemeni unity. The smaller GCC states did not usually pursue a policy directly opposed to that of Saudi Arabia.

There were two reasons for this, he explained. The first had to do with Yemen itself. In Qatar's judgment, Yemeni unity was very popular within Yemen while secession was not. Support for secession, then, was bound to fail and only result in arousing Yemeni animosity toward whomever supported it--both predictions which had come true.

The second had to do with Saudi-Qatari relations. Up until recently, he related, Qatar had been closer to Saudi Arabia than any other country. Qatar is the only other Muslim nation to share with the Saudis the strict Wahhabi interpretation of Islam. Qatar had always followed the Saudi lead in international relations up through the 1990-91 Gulf War, during which Qatari troops fought against Iraq.

In 1992, however, there was a border clash between Saudi Arabia and Qatar--something about which I had heard of but not read any detailed report on. Not surprisingly, Qatar blamed the Saudis. The Foreign Ministry official suggested that Saudi border guards had fired on their Qatari counterparts. What worried Doha was that Riyadh did not claim that this was an isolated event or try to smooth things over with Qatar. Instead, the Saudis used the occasion to reassert their claim to even more Qatari territory. Qatar, then, sympathized with Yemen which also has a border dispute with Saudi Arabia.

"The problem for us," he said, "is that while America is willing to go to great lengths to prevent nations like Iran and Iraq from harming Saudi Arabia, it isn't willing to do anything when the Saudis threaten their neighbors. In fact, Washington doesn't even want to acknowledge that this is happening."

"So what can you do?" I asked.

He shrugged his shoulders. "What can we do? We can talk about it. We can try to make friends in other countries, especially America. Maybe they can take actions that will either persuade or embarrass the Saudis into realizing that claiming our territory does nothing to advance their interests. We can't do much more than this."

* * *

Toward the end of our talk, my new friend seemed a little embarrassed. Finally, he said, "You know, there was a slight communication problem between our embassy in Washington and the ministry here about your visit. I only heard that you were coming just this very morning. Before you arrived, I placed a few calls to try to get you some other appointments, but was unable to make any."

My initial reaction, I am sorry to admit, was to feel irritated. But on reflection, I was amazed that the Foreign Ministry had been able to organize a VIP reception for me and at least one appointment on such short notice. There had been all too many Arab countries where I had been invited to visit only to discover that no reception or appointments had been arranged. Still, it was not clear how I was going to fill the almost twelve hours that remained before my onward flight.

My host made another round of phone calls for me, but to no avail. The work week in most Muslim countries goes from Saturday to Wednesday. I was in Doha on a Thursday. In Qatar, though, Thursday is also supposed to be a work day, but in many offices it has become part of the weekend while in others people usually leave by late morning.

But my friend's resourcefulness had not been exhausted. The chauffeur who had driven me from the airport to the ministry was assigned to me for the rest of the day. And despite my objections, my new friend insisted on providing me with a room at the Sheraton at the ministry's expense.

I asked my driver to take me on a tour of the city. He said that it would be better to do so in the late afternoon. During the height of the mid-day heat, he explained, almost everything closed down. So after checking me in at the hotel, we agreed to meet in the lobby at four. I had lunch and then went up to my room, which was an enormous, split-level suite. This was too much for one person, especially someone who was only staying a few hours.

* * *

After a short nap, I went back down to the vast lobby to look around before my driver arrived. I soon struck up a conversation with a Qatari named Fahd. I think he was about my age, though again it was difficult to tell when a man is wearing the traditional Arab headgear.

Fahd shared the distrust of the Saudis that I had heard at the Foreign Ministry. "The problem," said Fahd, "is that the Saudis are afraid of what modernization and Westernization will lead to. So they try to suppress all desire for change. But we in Qatar and the other smaller Gulf states know that change is inevitable. So we are trying to adapt slowly. But the Saudis don't like this. They think that if the countries most like them change, then they may not be able to avoid change themselves. And they seem to think that if they threaten our borders periodically, then somehow they will stop whatever change they don't like here. But of course they can't."

I asked him what sort of change was taking place in Qatar. "It's mainly in the economic sphere," he replied. "The boom days, when this hotel was built, are over. With the price of oil much lower than it was, we are economizing. Just because you're a Qatari man doesn't mean you're entitled to a highly paid job which involves little or no work. Now, you either earn your salary, or you will find yourself looking for another job.

"Our main problem, of course, is that there are so few Qataris. That is why you see so many foreign workers here. What we are trying to do, though, is train Qataris for jobs that require higher education. We don't want to have to rely on foreigners to do the most important jobs for us.

"We're so serious about this," he added, "that we have begun to integrate Qatari women into the work force. They are far more dedicated to building the country than foreigners are. A few years ago, Qatar was like Saudi Arabia: our women never worked beside our men. Now, they work in almost every ministry. And soon, they will work in them all."

Fahd seemed almost vehement about this. "So the women here are quite liberated?" I asked, looking at the few Qatari women in the lobby. All were covered in black and wearing veils.

Fahd laughed. "A few years ago, you wouldn't have seen them in a hotel lobby at all. And compared to Western women here, they dress very modestly. But at least they don't have to wear veils which cover their eyes, like in Saudi Arabia. Nor do they have to wear gloves. These may seem like little things to you, but to us they mean a great deal."

I asked him if the Qatari women he knew were satisfied with this. "That depends on how much time they've spent in the West," he answered. He told me about a Qatari girl whose parents had lived in London for most of her life. She dressed like a Western woman and went about by herself like one. When she turned eighteen, her parents moved back to Doha. At first, the parents let the girl behave like the many Western women living here: she wore what she liked and went out on her own. She even came to this hotel and sunbathed in her bikini like the foreign women. But when the girl's relatives found out, they put pressure on the parents to get her to behave traditionally. The parents complied to the point of confining their daughter to the house most of the time. They thought she would eventually adjust, but she didn't. After a couple of months, she told her parents that she couldn't live like this any more. If they didn't let her go back to London, she said she would kill herself. The parents let her go, and she hasn't been back since.

"And as far as I am concerned," said Fahd, "this story had a happy ending. I'm not sure it would have if she had been a Saudi girl.

"You know, Mark," he continued, "the problem for women in the Arab world is the attitude of the men. The men here think that if left on their own, women will not be able to control their behavior. They need to be protected by men constantly. But women don't need this protection. They can take care of themselves. And that is true whether they are covered in black like these ladies here, or are just wearing a bikini."

This is a viewpoint I had frequently heard expressed by Arab women, but almost never by an Arab man. If Fahd's attitude became widespread, relations between men and women in the Arab world would undergo a profound change.

* * *

I was just beginning to wonder where my driver was when I spotted him sitting on a couch in the lobby. It turned out that he had been there for some time, but did not want to interrupt my conversation. We got in the car and began our drive through the hot, dusty streets of Doha. Doha, like Abu Dhabi, was not a town with any old buildings--everything was new. I would later learn that there had been virtually nothing in Doha before oil was discovered. The Qataris had previously lived in tents.

We drove through the campus of the university. Everything, of course, was ultra-modern. From the signs, it soon became apparent that men and women were kept strictly segregated, attending classes in completely different buildings from each other. I concluded that Fahd's attitude toward women was not the prevailing one here.

Throughout the tour, my guide pointed out the homes of the amir, his son the heir apparent, and their many relatives. We passed by several houses belonging to the amir and the heir. I asked the driver why they each had so many right in town. "Each has three wives," the driver replied. He told me how the heir had just married his third wife. From his tone of voice, it was evident that the driver greatly admired him for this.

The following year (1995), the heir apparent would overthrow his father and become amir himself.

* * *

We drove to the Qatar National Museum, which was housed in a series of lovely white buildings which had won an Aga Khan prize for Islamic architecture. The first exhibit we looked at was a detailed display of the origins of Qatar's petroleum wealth, the various products it could be refined into, and where it was all located on land and off shore. Most of the exhibits, however, were devoted to life before oil. On display were examples of Qatari weaving, handicrafts, jewelry, weaponry, tents, and other items associated with daily life. There was an exhibit devoted to pearling--a grueling enterprise that served as one of the main sources of income for Qataris before oil.

Also on exhibit were rooms from the residences of previous amirs. What these showed were that even the rulers lived in relatively modest, uncomfortable circumstances before oil. One, in fact, had lived in a tent. On the whole, the museum exhibits conveyed the strong impression of just how difficult life was in this barren little country before oil made it wealthy. They also conveyed the impression that just to survive, Qataris had to be highly disciplined, hard-working, and self-reliant--qualities that had withstood the intense desert heat but had wilted as the country grew enormously wealthy from oil and natural gas.

After more sightseeing and some shopping, I was taken back to the VIP lounge at the airport. When the time came, I was driven in a Mercedes out to the awaiting Gulf Air jet to begin the long journey home.

Hopes and Fears

"Oil is a curse," she said. Her husband and brother nodded in agreement. We were having dinner at her home in Tehran.

"If we didn't have so much oil here in the Middle East," she continued, "maybe we would have developed normally, like other countries. But it is only our oil that Westerners care about, not the people here."

Oil is, indeed, the most important factor in the relations between the West on the one hand and the Middle East, especially the Persian Gulf region, on the other. For the basic fact regarding oil is that we need it, and they have it. And this will continue to be the case since the Persian Gulf region happens to possess most of the world's known petroleum reserves.

Our dependance on oil is the most important factor in how the U.S. and other Western governments view the Middle East. While the Arab-Israeli conflict has been the Middle Eastern news story that has captured the headlines over the years, what happens in the Persian Gulf is of far greater importance to Western economies. No matter how strong pro-Israeli and anti-Arab sentiment may have been within the American public and Congress in the past, Washington always took great care to ensure that relations with the oil rich monarchies of the Gulf remained close so that the oil would keep flowing. Far more dependant on Gulf oil than the U.S., other Western governments have worked assiduously to maintain good relations with those who supply them with it.

In the past few years, changes that once seemed impossible have come about. Communism has almost disappeared. The Soviet Union has dissolved. Israel and the Palestine Liberation Organization have signed a peace agreement and have made substantial progress toward implementing it. Democratization has spread to many countries.

But despite the dramatic changes occurring in so many parts of the world, even in the Arab-Israeli arena, the Muslim countries of the Middle East appear to be stuck in a political time warp. There has been almost no progress toward democracy in most of them. Further, while America and the West are actively promoting democratization elsewhere, they have not done so to any great extent in the Muslim Middle East--especially in the oil rich monarchies of the Arabian Peninsula. What is the obstacle here? As before, it is concern for oil.

Our main goal in the region is ensuring that oil continues to flow from it to the West. The fact that virulently anti-Western regimes are in power in both Iran and Iraq has heightened our concern about the Gulf monarchies. Due to our concern for their stability, we do not want to push for the democratization of these pro-Western regimes. For if we do, it is feared, something might go wrong in the process, resulting in pro-Western regimes being replaced by anti-Western ones which would limit or end our access to their oil. Indeed, our concern for the stability of the region's pro-Western regimes is so great that we do not even want to see anti-Western regimes democratized. For just the existence of a thriving democracy in Iran or Iraq could serve to undermine the authoritarian regimes in Saudi Arabia and the other oil rich monarchies of the Arabian Peninsula.

As change might negatively affect the supply of oil, we oppose all change in this part of the world. Instead, we back the status quo in Saudi Arabia and the other monarchies, telling ourselves that while they may not be democratic, they are surely better than the anti-Western radical nationalist or Islamic fundamentalist alternatives.

But the Muslim Middle East does not consist of oil alone. It also consists of people. Our concern for the supply of oil from the region has blinded us to the concerns of the people living there. We apparently assume that despite their lack of political or other freedoms, the people of Saudi Arabia and other countries with pro-Western regimes are so grateful for not living in worse places nearby such as Iraq that they will forever remain quiescent. But this is hardly realistic. Nowhere else in the world do we expect people to be satisfied living under authoritarian regimes. Do we really think that Muslims in the Middle East are somehow different from everyone else, that they alone want to be ruled by authoritarian regimes?

This presumption seems to be held only about Arabs and Persians. Muslims in some countries--Turkey, Pakistan, and Bangladesh--have made substantial progress toward democratization. Even when it has been interrupted in Turkey and Pakistan in the past, these countries have returned to democracy. Perhaps it is no coincidence that these three Muslim countries which have made the most progress toward democracy possess little or no oil.

It should be clear by now that the desire for democracy is a worldwide trend. If Americans and Westerners think that the Muslim Middle East is somehow immune to this trend, they are mistaken. Many people in this region also want democracy.

But, of course, there are also many people who want Islamic revolution in this part of the world. I don't mean to imply that Islam and democracy are incompatible. They are not, as Muslim democracies elsewhere have shown. There are many in the Arab world and Iran who also see Islam and democracy as compatible. Some believe that a true interpretation of Islam not only permits democracy, but actually requires it. These people, however, do not receive much attention in the West.

Those receiving the West's attention are the fundamentalists who advocate the killing of Westerners and the violent overthrow of the regimes in power. The sad fact about these zealots and their supporters is that so many of them actually think that what they are doing is democratic. Denied the opportunity to compete for power democratically, they feel justified in attempting to seize it undemocratically instead. Unfortunately, Islamic forces that come to power this way are not likely to be led by democratic elements, but by leaders who will establish a dictatorship of their own--as the many Iranians who opposed the shah learned after he was replaced by Ayatollah Khomeini.

The situation we now see in much of the Arab world is a triangular contest in which authoritarian governments face opposition both from democratic forces and from radical Islamic ones. The regime receives assistance from the West which fears Islamic radicals. The Islamic radicals, in turn, receive aid from Iran, Sudan, Afghanistan, and a number of other sources in the Islamic revolutionary movement. The democrats receive support from nobody.

This is a recipe for disaster. For if the recent past has taught us anything, its lesson is that authoritarian regimes eventually fall. If the Islamic fundamentalists are the only ones receiving external assistance, then they-- not the democrats--are the ones likely to come to power when this occurs.

Can this process be stopped? Perhaps it could if we strongly encouraged pro-Western regimes to democratize and supported democratic groups in these countries. But even if Western governments did recognize that unpopular authoritarian regimes are unstable in the long run (or in the short run in some cases), it is doubtful that the Middle Eastern rulers we support would permit a process that would lead to their being voted out of office. Even if they were willing, it might be too late. The fundamentalists are now so strong in many countries that they could easily defeat what little of the unarmed democratic opposition remains which the existing governments have not already destroyed. And as much as Western governments fear the Islamic fundamentalists, Western publics and parliaments are highly unlikely to countenance major military intervention in the Middle East to prevent them from coming to power. Thus, when the existing regimes become increasingly unpopular and inevitably fall, we may be powerless to prevent them from being supplanted by anti-Western, authoritarian Islamic regimes throughout the Muslim Middle East.

I have never been known, I must admit, for being an optimist. And what I have depicted here is definitely a pessimistic scenario. Yet amidst all this pessimism, I see two reasons for optimism about the Muslim Middle East and its relations with the West.

First, despite the all-consuming American concern about keeping friendly regimes in power in the Persian Gulf to ensure the continued supply of oil to the West, there is no reason to think that anti-Western regimes would not sell it to us. Virulently anti-Western regimes in Iraq, Iran, and Libya have all sold as much oil as they could to the West. It is the United States, either with its allies or (more usually) alone, which has refused to buy it. And the reason anti-Western states sell oil to the West is clear: they need money. This is not likely to change.

Second, and more profoundly, it was my visit to Iran in 1992 that gave me the greatest cause for optimism. For Iran in the early 1990s reminded me very much of the Soviet Union in the early 1980s. Enthusiasm for the revolution had largely disappeared. People had long realized that the revolutionary regime was incapable of making life better for them. Disaffection and disillusionment were widespread not only within the general population, but the ruling regime itself. And as the demise of Marxist regimes in Eastern Europe, the Soviet Union, and the Third World demonstrated, anti-Western authoritarian governments eventually fall just as do pro-Western ones.

Ironically, enthusiasm for Islamic revolution is growing in the Arab countries where it has not yet occurred just as disillusion with this form of revolution has become increasingly widespread in Iran, the country having the most experience with it. This is similar to the 1970s when enthusiasm for Marxist revolution was at its height in Third World countries which had not experienced it just as disillusion with it was growing tremendously in Brezhnev's USSR.

Revolution--whether Islamic or Marxist--may be like a fever: nations catch it, but it eventually burns itself out. The good news from the Marxist experience is that when the revolutionary fever finally does burn out, it can give rise to democracy. The bad news is that the burning out process can take decades to complete. In the meantime, the people forced to live through this process suffer enormously.

Mark N. Katz is an associate professor of government and politics at George Mason University in Fairfax, Virginia. He received a B.A. in international relations from the University of California at Riverside in 1976, an M.A. in international relations from the Johns Hopkins University School of Advanced International Studies in 1978, and a Ph.D. in political science from the Massachusetts Institute of Technology in 1982. He is the author of *Revolutions and Revolutionary Waves* (St. Martin's Press, 1997), and many other scholarly publications. He has also contributed travel narratives to *The National Interest* and *Middle East Quarterly* as well as a short story to *Twisted Roots Literary Magazine*.